Training Manual for Behavior Technicians Working with Individuals with Autism

Training Manual for Behavior Technicians Working with Individuals with Autism

Jonathan Tarbox
Courtney Tarbox

AMSTERDAM • BOSTON • HEIDELBERG • LONDON
NEW YORK • OXFORD • PARIS • SAN DIEGO
SAN FRANCISCO • SINGAPORE • SYDNEY • TOKYO
Academic Press is an imprint of Elsevier

Academic Press is an imprint of Elsevier
125 London Wall, London EC2Y 5AS, United Kingdom
525 B Street, Suite 1800, San Diego, CA 92101-4495, United States
50 Hampshire Street, 5th Floor, Cambridge, MA 02139, United States
The Boulevard, Langford Lane, Kidlington, Oxford OX5 1GB, United Kingdom

British Library Cataloguing-in-Publication Data
A catalogue record for this book is available from the British Library

Library of Congress Cataloging-in-Publication Data
A catalog record for this book is available from the Library of Congress

ISBN: 978-0-12-809408-2

For Information on all Academic Press publications
visit our website at https://www.elsevier.com

  Working together
to grow libraries in
developing countries

ELSEVIER · Book Aid International

www.elsevier.com • www.bookaid.org

Publisher: Nikki Levy
Acquisition Editor: Emily Ekle
Editorial Project Manager: Barbara Makinster
Production Project Manager: Sruthi Satheesh
Cover Designer: Mark Roger

Typeset by MPS Limited, Chennai, India
Transferred to Digital Printing 2016

CONTENTS

BIOGRAPHIES

Jonathan Tarbox, PhD, BCBA-D, is the Program Director of the Master of Science in Applied Behavior Analysis program at the University of Southern California, as well as Director of Research and a Regional Clinic Director at FirstSteps for Kids. He is associate editor of the journal *Behavior Analysis in Practice* and serves on the editorial boards of five major scientific journals related to autism and behavior analysis. He has published two previous books on autism treatment and well over 70 peer-reviewed journal articles and chapters in scientific texts. His research focuses on behavioral interventions for teaching complex skills to individuals with autism. He is a frequent presenter at autism and ABA conferences worldwide, and a regular guest on television and radio.

Courtney Tarbox, MS, BCBA, is a Regional Clinic Director at FirstSteps for Kids, an ABA service provider offering comprehensive intervention to children on the autism spectrum. Her early work in developmental disabilities included working in therapeutic, residential, and educational settings, with individuals diagnosed with a variety of developmental disorders and ranging in age from early childhood to adolescence. She has worked at FirstSteps since 2009 and is responsible for designing and overseeing individualized treatment plans that are unique to each child's needs, as well as monitoring the service provision implemented by behavior technicians to ensure that competent and dedicated individuals are providing intervention leading to meaningful progress for the children with whom they work. She is actively engaged in treatment evaluation research and has published in peer-reviewed journals. She is a regular presenter at autism and ABA conferences and gives parent and community presentations with the aim of dispelling common misconceptions about ABA treatment for children with autism.

ACKNOWLEDGMENTS

We would like to thank Dr. Shawn Quigley, Thea Davis, and Demetria Contreras for their input on the content of this book, as well as their generous sharing of behavior technician training resources they have developed. We thank Taira Bermudez for her thoughtful input and guidance on versions of the manuscript. We thank Dr. Jennifer Harris and Lisa Stoddard, for sharing clinical resources used in this book and for creating and leading an incredible organization, FirstSteps for Kids, Inc., that encourages behavior analysts to thrive. We thank our editors at Elsevier, Emily Ekle, and Barbara Makinster, for their guidance on this and the other books we have worked on together. We would like to especially thank our moms, T. Carole Eden and Melody Riggs, for their help with proofreading. We want to thank Jamie Nicole Scott and the rest of the incredible photographers at Spectrum Inspired for the beautiful cover image. Their dedication to documenting the beauty in the everyday experiences of children with autism and their families is truly inspiring. To learn more, visit www. spectruminspired.org.

We dedicate this book to current and future generations of behavior technicians who choose to make their lives about helping families affected by autism. Your dedication means more than you know.

CHAPTER 1

Introduction

Applied behavior analysis (ABA) is a science that uses principles of learning and motivation that have come from decades of scientific research to solve problems of behavior that matter to society. In order to address the most important problems, several levels of practitioners are often needed. ABA services are generally overseen by a master's (BCBA®) or PhD (BCBA-D®) level Board Certified Behavior Analyst®, may receive mid-level oversight by a bachelors level (BCaBA®) practitioner, and are implemented directly by Registered Behavior Technicians (RBT™). Behavior technicians are the ones that work directly with the learners and they are the ones whose behavior most directly affects client outcome. Therefore, when you are working in your future job as a behavior technician, you are going to be the tip of the spear. The job of the behavior technician is hugely important and has tremendous responsibility, but the benefits of the job are truly remarkable. In a very real way, your job will make a meaningful difference in the life of someone every day.

Our goal in writing this manual is to provide a written text to be used as part of a 40-hour training program that is based on the *Registered Behavior Technician (RBT) Task List* (Behavior Analyst Certification Board, 2013) and is designed to meet the training requirements for the RBT credential. You should print out the task list and refer to it regularly while you read this book and take your training. It is important to note that this book and any training program that it is used as a part of is offered independently of the Behavior Analyst Certification Board® and is not affiliated with or endorsed by the Board in any way.

1.1 FORMAT OF THE BOOK

This book contains seven chapters. You are reading Chapter 1 right now and we hope your interest is already captured. Chapter 2, Autism

Training Manual for Behavior Technicians Working with Individuals with Autism.
DOI: http://dx.doi.org/10.1016/B978-0-12-809408-2.00001-5

Spectrum Disorder, gives you introductory information about autism and ABA and an overview of ABA treatment for autism. Chapter 3, Measurement and Data Collection, teaches you some of the many ways that you will use data collection to measure behavior. Chapter 4, Assessment, teaches you how you will assist your supervisor in assessing behavior. Chapter 5, Skill Acquisition, is the longest and most important chapter because it explains how to teach new skills to individuals with autism spectrum disorder (ASD). Chapter 6, Behavior Reduction, teaches you how to decrease challenging behaviors. Chapter 7, Documentation and Professional Conduct, the final chapter, covers professional issues that are critical to your daily practice as a behavior technician.

In this training manual we are going to teach you to speak in a few different languages. First, we are going to teach you the meaning behind the concepts that you need to learn to perform excellently as a behavior technician and to pass the RBT examination. Second, we are going to teach you the technical definition of those terms. Finally, we are going to teach you how to explain those terms to a nontechnical audience. You will notice that we use very plain language and we make no attempt to sound technical or scholarly. For example, we often write something like "...do the behavior" instead of "...execute the response" or "...having a tantrum" instead of "...engaging in tantrum behavior." We made this choice of language deliberately because the goal of this book is to teach you the meaning behind the principles and procedures of behavior analysis, not to teach you technically and scientifically perfect language. There is a reason and purpose for technically precise language and we have published other books and articles that are good resources for learning such language. After you achieve your RBT credential and are ready for more training, we encourage you to read *Applied Behavior Analysis* (Cooper et al., 2007) and *Handbook of Early Intervention for Autism Spectrum Disorders: Research, Policy, and Practice* (Tarbox, Dixon, Sturmey, & Matson, 2014). For now, we invite you to not worry too much about sounding smart and just focus on learning the meaning behind the many new principles and procedures you are about to be trained in. Similarly, we intentionally left out references to research articles throughout this book. If you are interested, the two books cited above contain thousands of scientific references and including them in this book would only make it less readable.

1.2 A BRIEF NOTE ON STUDYING WITH THIS BOOK

A large amount of research has shown that people learn best when they are taught many different examples of a concept. This is called *multiple exemplar training* (see section on generalization in chapter: Skill Acquisition) and it works as well for teaching learners with ASD as it does for training adult staff members like you. This book is intentionally written to give you terms, the definitions of those terms, and then multiple examples that illustrate the concept. In order to make the learning experience most effective, you should try to create at least three of your own new examples for every new term in the book. If there are other trainees who are being trained with you, we recommend you form study groups and quiz each other. But more important than memorizing the terms, you should quiz each other on the ability to create new examples. You will know you have mastered a concept when you can create new examples with ease. You can start this process right now with the remaining concepts in this chapter.

1.3 SEVEN DIMENSIONS OF ABA

Three of the founding fathers of ABA, Baer, Wolf, and Risley, published a discussion article in 1968 that defined and discussed seven dimensions that characterized the field of ABA. Forty-eight years later, these same seven dimensions continue to define ABA and it is well worth it to learn them and consider them on a daily basis as you work as a behavior technician.

1.3.1 Applied
The field of ABA focuses on changing behaviors that are important to society. The principles and procedures of ABA are powerful and could be used to change just about any behavior, but we believe it is important to use our limited amount of time and resources to improve the behaviors that matter the most.

1.3.2 Behavioral
Our subject matter is behavior and behavior includes everything people say and do. We focus on observable behavior because that is what we can measure and that is where we can make a difference. For example, we focus on decreasing aggression much more than we focus on anger,

we focus on increasing exercise more than increasing feelings of self-efficacy, and we focus on decreasing smoking more than decreasing urges to smoke.

1.3.3 Analytic

We analyze the ways in which changes in a person's environment affect their behavior and we strive to demonstrate this through careful and systematic manipulation of the environment to observe changes in behavior. We carefully measure behavior before and after intervention and we sometimes (especially in research) use experimental designs to demonstrate how environment controls behavior. We attempt to rule out all other possible explanations for behavior change. We are skeptical of our own effectiveness and we want to know what really works. We hold our procedures accountable for their effectiveness.

1.3.4 Conceptually Systematic

We strive to understand the effects of everything we do in terms of the basic principles of learning and motivation that come from decades of research in behavior analysis. It is not enough to merely notice that a procedure works. We strive to understand why it works in terms of behavioral principles. Becoming fluent at understanding all of human behavior in terms of behavioral principles takes a lifetime of practice, but you will immediately start to recognize examples of all of the principles discussed in this book in your daily life. Thinking like this will help you understand why what we do with learners with autism works and it will help you troubleshoot what to do when things are not working.

1.3.5 Effective

The goal of ABA is to produce *substantial* changes in behaviors that matter. We are not interested in a *statistically significant* effect if it did not make a meaningful difference in the learner's life. For example, decreasing hitting oneself from 100 times per day to 90 times per day is better than nothing. But if one is still hitting oneself 90 times per day, the problem is not solved. An ABA intervention would be expected to decrease the behavior to a level that is reasonable for the client to live with on a daily basis.

1.3.6 Generalized Outcomes

The goal of ABA is to produce important behavior changes that generalize to all relevant aspects of a learner's life (see section on generalization in chapter: Skill Acquisition). For example, if a child was only potty trained at school but not at home, the problem would clearly not be solved. The lack of generalization from school to home would be considered unacceptable and intervention would need to be continued until the individual is continent in all settings.

1.3.7 Technological

In scientific terms, technological means that a procedure is described clearly enough so that other people could replicate it (it does not mean computer technology). This is important because if ABA procedures are not clearly described, it will not be possible for others to learn from them and to use them with the clients with whom they work.

1.4 FOUNDATIONAL PRINCIPLES

In this section, we provide brief technical definitions and examples of core concepts and principles that are critical for your training. Keep in mind this list is not comprehensive of all concepts and principles in ABA, but it contains the most foundational ones that will be important to your understanding of the content in the rest of the book. Don't worry if you do not feel completely confident in your understanding of these terms when you are finished reading this section. It is meant to be a brief first introduction and all of the terms are covered in more depth throughout the book. To get the most out of this section, we recommend you make flashcards of the terms below and find a fellow behavior technician trainee to study with. You should spend a lot of time training each other to fluency. A great way to do this is to practice the following four different types of exercises, where one trainee provides the first part and the other trainee provides the second part: (1) Term—Definition, (2) Definition—Term, (3) Term—Example, (4) Example—Term. Continue practicing with each other until you both can perform quickly and accurately on all four types of drills and where you and your fellow trainee can do exercise 3 and 4 with new examples that you were never trained on. That is, you can create new examples of terms and you can identify the correct term when someone provides you with a new example you have never heard before. Here are the terms you will need to learn:

1.4.1 Behavior
Anything a person says or does. Also known as a response. Examples include saying "Can I have some water, please?", hitting someone, crying, washing your hands, playing with a toy, reading a book, and so on.

1.4.2 Stimulus
Any object or event that occurs in a person's environment. For something to count as a stimulus for a particular person at a particular time, that person has to have seen, heard, touched, tasted, or smelled that object or event. Examples include the sight of an apple, a loud noise, the smell of cookies, someone saying "Hi" to you, and so on.

1.4.3 Antecedent
A stimulus that occurred in a person's environment immediately preceding a behavior. For example, a child's mother says, "Time to turn off the TV" and the child has a tantrum. When considering the child's behavior, the mother asking him to turn off the television is the antecedent and the tantrum is the child's behavior.

1.4.4 Consequence
A stimulus that occurred in a person's environment immediately following a behavior. For example, a child has a tantrum and gets candy. The tantrum is the behavior and the candy is the consequence. Consequence in ABA terms does *not* mean what it means in everyday usage, where consequence implies negative consequence or punishment. In ABA terms, a consequence can be either preferred, nonpreferred, or neutral. It simply means whatever happened immediately after behavior.

1.4.5 Positive Reinforcement
A consequence of a behavior that involves adding something to the person's environment, which increases the future strength of that behavior. For example, a learner says, "Hug please," gets a hug, and then is more likely to say, "Hug please" the next time he wants a hug. Saying, "Hug please" is the behavior and getting a hug is the positive reinforcer that strengthened that behavior.

1.4.6 Negative Reinforcement

A consequence of a behavior that involves removing something from or postponing something in the person's environment, which increases the future strength of that behavior. For example, a child with autism says, "Break please," his teacher removes his work, and he is then more likely to say, "Break please" the next time he wants a break. Saying, "Break please" is the behavior and having work removed is the negative reinforcer that strengthens that behavior. Note that the term "negative" simply means something was removed, it does not mean negative as in bad or undesirable. Contrary to popular belief, negative reinforcement does *not* mean punishment.

1.4.7 Motivating Operation

An antecedent that changes the potency of a consequence as a reinforcer. Motivating operations are divided into two types: (1) Establishing operations and (2) abolishing operations. Establishing operations increase the potency of a consequence as a reinforcer and temporarily evoke behavior. For example, if an adult with autism has not eaten in a few hours, food becomes a stronger reinforcer and she is likely to ask for food or do other behaviors that have gotten her food in the past.

Abolishing operations decrease the potency of a consequence as a reinforcer and temporarily suppress behavior. For example, if an adolescent with autism has just finished a large glass of water, water is no longer a powerful reinforcer at that moment and she is not likely to ask for water. Later on, if she has not had water again for a long time, then the lack of water will be an establishing operation, which makes water a powerful reinforcer again.

1.4.8 Extinction

No longer providing reinforcement for a behavior that used to be reinforced, resulting in a decrease in that behavior in the future. For example, if a child had tantrums in order to avoid cleaning her room, and her mother no longer allows her to escape from cleaning her room when she has a tantrum, then tantrums decrease in the future. In another example, if an adult with ASD who lives in a group home uses appropriate communication to try to get the attention of a staff member, but the staff member does not respond, then the person with autism is less likely to use appropriate communication to get her attention in the future.

1.4.9 Stimulus Control

When a behavior is reinforced in the presence of a particular antecedent stimulus and is not reinforced in the absence of that stimulus, the behavior comes to occur reliably in the presence of that stimulus. For example, if a child's grandmother usually gives a child candy when the child asks for it (i.e., reinforces the behavior of asking for candy by giving the child candy), then the child will reliably ask for candy when grandma comes over.

1.4.10 Discriminative Stimulus

A discriminative stimulus is the antecedent stimulus that has stimulus control over behavior because the behavior was reliably reinforced in the presence of that stimulus in the past. Discriminative stimuli set the occasion for behaviors that have been reinforced in their presence in the past. In the example above, the grandma is the discriminative stimulus for the behavior of asking for candy. In nontechnical terms, a discriminative stimulus tells the person what behavior is going to get reinforced—it signals the availability of a particular reinforcer for a particular behavior. The abbreviation for discriminative stimulus is "Sd."

1.4.11 Generalization

The spreading of the effects of intervention to outside of the intervention. For example, a behavior technician teaches a child with autism to share when playing with toys with the technician and then the child shares her toys when she plays with her brother.

1.4.12 Prompt

An extra antecedent stimulus that helps a person engage in a particular behavior. Hints and cues are examples of prompts. For example, when teaching a child with autism her name, a behavior technician asks the child "What is your name?" and then models it for her by saying "Andrea." In this example, when the behavior technician says "Andrea," it is a prompt. By definition, prompts are extra help that you want to fade out as soon as possible, so learners do not become dependent on them.

The small number of basic terms listed above form the foundation for what you need to learn to become an RBT. In fact, by applying these basic concepts to learning, motivation, and behavior, you can understand and teach an amazing variety of skills to learners with autism and have a profound positive impact on the ability of others to lead meaningful, independent lives. With the tools you are about to learn, you are launching on a career of making a difference, one person at a time.

CHAPTER 2

Autism Spectrum Disorder

The Registered Behavior Technician (RBT) Task List does not contain information on any particular disorder because the RBT credential is not designed for behavior technicians that work with any particular population. Therefore, the exam does not contain any information on autism, nor are behavior technician trainees required to learn any information specific to autism for the RBT exam. However, if you are reading this book, you are likely going to be working with individuals with autism so we believe it will be useful for you to learn some foundational knowledge of the disorder. If you are reading this book solely to learn the behavioral content and study for the exam or if you do not work with individuals with autism, feel free to skip this chapter and move on to Chapter 3, Measurement and Data Collection.

2.1 HISTORY AND BACKGROUND OF AUTISM

Autism was originally identified by Leo Kanner in 1943. Kanner described 11 children who were intelligent but had significant challenges in relating to and connecting with others. The condition was originally named "early infantile autism." Autism was very rare at the time and little was known about its causes. Infamously, Bruno Bettelheim, a child psychologist in the 1960s, who was actually trained in art history, espoused a theory of autism called the "refrigerator mother" theory. The refrigerator mother theory stated that autism is caused by parents, especially mothers, who were emotionally cold and unattached to their babies. This theory was obviously ridiculous from the very start because families that had one child with autism very often had other children who did not have autism even though the parents treated them all in much the same way. Even though the refrigerator mother theory was ill conceived from the beginning, it was widely believed and it was many years before it was discredited. As a result, an entire generation of parents were made to feel terribly guilty by others who assumed that they had caused their child's autism. The

Training Manual for Behavior Technicians Working with Individuals with Autism.
DOI: http://dx.doi.org/10.1016/B978-0-12-809408-2.00002-7

unfortunate results of this irresponsible theory lasted decades, and to this day, it is very common for parents of children with autism to feel like some part of their child's autism must be their fault. Fortunately, all experts now agree that, although parent behavior has an effect on child behavior for children with autism (just as it does for all children), *parenting does not cause autism.*

When autism was first identified it was extremely rare but, the incidence and prevalence of autism have grown dramatically since. As of the time this manual was written, the US Centers for Disease Control and Prevention estimate that one in every 68 US children has ASD. Many aspects of the autism diagnosis have changed over the decades. In addition, awareness of the disorder has increased as well as availability of funding for treatment of the disorder. All of these factors likely contribute to the increasing prevalence of autism, but most experts agree that some substantial portion of the increase is also real. Hundreds of theories of the causes of autism exist but none have been proven on any large scale and we will not cover any here. Right now, when someone asks you what causes autism, the only scientifically responsible answer remains, "We honestly still do not know."

2.2 DIAGNOSTIC CRITERIA

The diagnostic criteria for autism have changed substantially over the last few decades. Until recently, several different "pervasive developmental disorders" formed a spectrum of different autism disorders, including Autistic Disorder, Pervasive Developmental Disorder Not Otherwise Specified, and Asperger's Disorder. When the DSM 5 was published in 2013 (the most recent version of the manual that specifies diagnostic criteria), a single disorder replaced those three disorders (American Psychiatric Association, 2013). Autism is now referred to as autism spectrum disorder (ASD) and includes the full spectrum of individuals, ranging from individuals who are severely affected (formerly referred to as having autistic disorder), to individuals who are mildly affected (formerly referred to as having Asperger's disorder), and everyone in between. Although the official name of the disorder is now ASD, it is very common to simply say autism and we use the terms "autism" and "ASD" interchangeably in this book. You will also likely meet people who were diagnosed before 2013 and may therefore have one of the older diagnoses.

2.2.1 DSM 5 Criteria

The following language is quoted directly from the American Psychiatric Association's *Diagnostic and Statistical Manual of Mental Disorders, Fifth Edition: DSM 5* (American Psychiatric Association, 2013).

1. Persistent deficits in social communication and social interaction across multiple contexts, as manifested by the following, currently or by history (examples are illustrative, not exhaustive, see text):
   a. Deficits in social-emotional reciprocity, ranging, e.g., from abnormal social approach and failure of normal back-and-forth conversation; to reduced sharing of interests, emotions, or affect; to failure to initiate or respond to social interactions.
   b. Deficits in nonverbal communicative behaviors used for social interaction, ranging, e.g., from poorly integrated verbal and non-verbal communication; to abnormalities in eye contact and body language or deficits in understanding and use of gestures; to a total lack of facial expressions and nonverbal communication.
   c. Deficits in developing, maintaining, and understanding relation-ships, ranging, e.g., from difficulties adjusting behavior to suit various social contexts; to difficulties in sharing imaginative play or in making friends; to absence of interest in peers.
2. Restricted, repetitive patterns of behavior, interests, or activities, as manifested by at least two of the following, currently or by history (examples are illustrative, not exhaustive; see text):
   a. Stereotyped or repetitive motor movements, use of objects, or speech (e.g., simple motor stereotypies, lining up toys or flipping objects, echolalia, idiosyncratic phrases).
   b. Insistence on sameness, inflexible adherence to routines, or ritu-alized patterns of verbal or nonverbal behavior (e.g., extreme distress at small changes, difficulties with transitions, rigid think-ing patterns, greeting rituals, need to take same route or eat same food every day).
   c. Highly restricted, fixated interests that are abnormal in intensity or focus (e.g., strong attachment to or preoccupation with unusual objects, excessively circumscribed or perseverative interest).
   d. Hyper- or hyporeactivity to sensory input or unusual interests in sensory aspects of the environment (e.g., apparent indifference to pain/temperature, adverse response to specific sounds or tex-tures, excessive smelling or touching of objects, visual fascination with lights or movement).

3. Symptoms must be present in the early developmental period (but may not become fully manifest until social demands exceed limited capacities, or may be masked by learned strategies in later life).
4. Symptoms cause clinically significant impairment in social, occupational, or other important areas of current functioning.
5. These disturbances are not better explained by intellectual disability (intellectual developmental disorder) or global developmental delay. Intellectual disability and autism spectrum disorder frequently cooccur; to make comorbid diagnoses of autism spectrum disorder and intellectual disability, social communication should be below that expected for general developmental level.

2.2.2 Severity
In addition to showing the symptoms listed in criteria A and B above, the diagnosing medical doctor or psychologist will often provide a severity rating for both symptom areas, ranging from Level 1 (requiring support) to Level 3 (requiring very substantial support).

2.2.3 Who Can Diagnose
In the United States, only medical doctors or licensed psychologists are permitted to diagnose someone with autism. School district staff will often assess students and can identify whether they meet eligibility to receive special education services due to autism symptoms, but these designations generally do not qualify as official medical diagnoses.

2.2.4 Every Individual With Autism Is Different
Perhaps the most important thing you need to know about autism is that every individual with autism is different. Forget all of the myths and rumors you have heard and forget all of the movies you have seen. Those stereotypes only apply to a very small percentage of people with ASD. What matters the most is for us to figure out what particular skills any particular learner needs to learn and how to motivate her to learn them. The answer to these questions will be different with every learner you work with and it is the BCBA's job to create a plan based on these factors and to train you on how to implement it. The rest of this manual describes the type of work you will be doing to implement these plans.

Although every individual with autism is different, there are some common defining features that are characteristic of the diagnosis. For example, persistent deficits in social communication skills are a core symptom that applies to all individuals with autism. On the more severe end of the spectrum, this can manifest in a complete absence of basic social skills, such as eye contact, greetings, or sharing. On the more mild end of the spectrum, an individual may have many foundational social skills, such as sharing, turn taking, and basic conversational skills, but may have no ability to understand the thoughts, beliefs, intentions, or emotions of others (i.e., perspective taking). Therefore, the specific target social skills that you might teach on any given day are going to vary dramatically from learner to learner, and yet the overall goal of teaching all of these social skills is to help the learner connect to the social world and find enjoyment in it. So, while you will prompt and reinforce very different social behaviors with different learners, the overall goal is the same: to enhance social functioning and to teach the learner that the social world is a source of positive reinforcement.

Restricted and repetitive interests is another core diagnostic feature that is common to all individuals with ASD. Again, this symptom will be completely different from person to person. On the more severe end of the spectrum, a learner may engage in repetitive motor behaviors (e.g., hand flapping or rocking) during most of her free time. On the more mild end of the spectrum, a learner may insist on talking about the same obscure conversational topic (e.g., engine statistics) repeatedly, despite others becoming bored with it. So again, the specific repetitive behaviors that you will help the learner decrease will be different with every learner. But the overarching goal is the same: we are trying to teach learners with autism to tolerate behaving flexibly, doing things differently, and being open to change. Put more broadly, we are trying to teach individuals with ASD to enjoy the variability that is a normal part of everyday life, rather than insisting on sameness.

2.3 ABA TREATMENT FOR AUTISM

Applied behavior analysis (ABA) treatment for autism has been supported by several decades of scientific research, resulting in close to 1000 published studies (National Autism Center, 2015). In addition to this chapter, *Applied Behavior Analysis Treatment for Autism Spectrum Disorder: Practice Guidelines for Healthcare Funders and Managers* (Behavior Analyst Certification Board, 2014a) is a very useful resource. The general idea behind ABA treatment for autism is to help individuals with autism achieve their greatest potential by decreasing challenging behaviors and teaching skills that help foster empowerment, happiness, and independence. ABA treatment for ASD takes many different forms, but most can be classified as either (1) comprehensive treatment, or (2) focused treatment.

2.3.1 Comprehensive Treatment

Comprehensive treatment for individuals with autism is designed to address all major areas of skill deficits and all challenging behaviors that a particular individual has. Therefore, comprehensive treatment programs usually address all major areas of human development, including language, social skills, play skills, independent living skills, motor skills, and academic skills. Some more advanced ABA programs also address perspective taking skills and executive function skills. Comprehensive treatment programs are usually implemented *intensively*, which means that the learner receives 25–40 hours per week of one-to-one treatment. Research has shown that this treatment approach produces the largest gains when started as early as possible, at least before 3.5 years old. However, as soon as the child receives the autism diagnosis, treatment should begin and has been started when the learner is as young as 18 months of age. Comprehensive ABA treatment that is done for 25 or more hours per week, starting before the age of 3.5 years, and continuing for at least 2 or more years, is called *early intensive behavioral intervention (EIBI)*.

2.3.2 Focused Treatment

Focused ABA treatment has a much narrower scope than comprehensive treatment in that it focuses on one or a few specific challenging behaviors or skill deficits as the target of treatment. For example, you might work in a program with the primary purpose of decreasing severe challenging behaviors and replacing them with more appropriate replacement behaviors, such as communication. Similarly, some ABA programs focus primarily on social skills, feeding disorders, job training skills, academic tutoring, or independent living skills, such as toileting. In the vast majority of such cases, the learner with autism has many other skill deficits that are not being addressed by the focused program. Focused treatment programs vary in weekly intensity (i.e., hours per week) and in total duration (i.e., weeks, months, or years of treatment) but are, by definition, less intensive and shorter in duration than comprehensive programs. Ideally, the intensity of the focused program should be determined by how severe the problem is and the duration should be determined by how long it actually takes to solve the problem. However, the unfortunate reality is that the weekly intensity and overall duration are usually determined by funding agencies, such as health insurance plans, state developmental disability funding agencies, and school districts.

2.3.3 General Philosophy of ABA Programs

Some basic philosophical assumptions of ABA treatment programs for learners with autism are worth mentioning because they shape the decisions we make on a daily basis and they provide us with daily inspiration and hope.

Everyone with autism is capable of learning. We believe that all individuals with autism can learn. Some learn more rapidly than others, but there is no way to determine that beforehand and regardless, that fact should not affect any individual's access to treatment. We have no idea how much any individual with ASD is capable of learning, but we are 100% sure that, however much she knows today, she can know a little bit more tomorrow.

Right to effective treatment. We believe that all individuals with autism have a right to effective treatment. The fact that treatment is expensive or difficult to access does not affect the moral obligation that we, as a society, have to provide effective treatment for autism, just like any other disorder.

The learner is always right. In ABA, we believe that good teaching causes good learning. So if a behavioral intervention procedure or teaching procedure is not working, we blame the procedure, not the learner. The fact that someone has autism or intellectual disability is not an excuse for an ineffective treatment or education plan. Our job in ABA is to continue to modify and innovate treatment procedures until we find a procedure that works.

Self-Determination. We believe that individuals with autism, just like any other human being, have a right to determine their own destiny and be the masters of their own lives, to the greatest extent possible. For this reason, ABA treatment should never be forced on a family. The purpose of ABA treatment is to help people in need achieve what they want in life, not to force anyone into being "normal" or conforming to society.

Least intrusive treatment. We believe that individuals with ASD, like any other disorder, have a right to receive the least intrusive treatment possible. What this means is that physical force should never be used above and beyond what is necessary to protect safety. Reinforcement-based procedures should always be used and sufficiently exhausted prior to considering restrictive or punitive measures. In addition, individuals with autism should be included in regular, nonrestricted, nonsecluded settings to the greatest extent possible, as long as safety and effective learning can be ensured.

CHAPTER 3

Measurement and Data Collection

Collecting data on the behaviors of clients, parents, and other caregivers is an important part of working as a behavior technician. It is critical to collect data and document the progress your clients make because everyday human experience and science has proven for centuries that human memory alone is not reliable. Consider the role of stats in competitive sports. Every professional football player, baseball player, basketball player, and so on has nearly every important aspect of their performance scored, analyzed, and recorded on a regular basis. The reason for this is so that the players get immediate and precise feedback on their performance so that they can determine whether they are improving, staying the same, or getting worse. The same is true for the learners with autism with whom you are going to work. It is the responsibility of the team of behavior technicians to constantly assess the progress of the learner. When working as a behavior technician, you will record a wide variety of data on learner behavior. In this chapter, we describe how to prepare for data collection and how to carry out the most common types of data collection that you will be responsible for in your job. As you read through this chapter, sample datasheets are provided with hypothetical data to illustrate what you are learning.

3.1 PREPARATION FOR DATA COLLECTION

You should spend a few minutes getting ready to collect data before you are expected to do it. Here is a checklist of what to do each time in order to make sure you are ready:

1. The first thing you need to do is consult whatever skill acquisition plan or behavior reduction plan you are collecting data for, in order to make sure you know what behaviors you are collecting data on and what data collection methods you need to use.
2. Gather the materials you need to collect data. At the time this manual is being written, most behavior technicians still use pens and

Training Manual for Behavior Technicians Working with Individuals with Autism.
DOI: http://dx.doi.org/10.1016/B978-0-12-809408-2.00003-9

paper datasheets to collect data. Within a few years, this will likely not be the case. So, whether you are using pen and paper or a tablet or smartphone or some other device to collect data, get the materials you will need ready.

3. Write or enter in the learner's name, date, the particular skill acquisition or behavior intervention plan being conducted, and any other specific information that your supervising BCBA designates.

4. Take any necessary measures to eliminate or minimize distractions that might hinder your attention to the behavior that you need to observe (e.g., music, television, etc.).

5. You are ready to collect data. Keep your eyes on the learner and stay sharp!

3.2 CONTINUOUS MEASUREMENT

Generally speaking, continuous measurement of behavior is preferred over discontinuous measurement because *continuous measurement* records all of the behavior as it actually occurs during an observation, not an estimate of it. Frequency and duration recording are the most important types of continuous measurement for you to learn.

3.2.1 Frequency

The simplest way to directly measure behavior is to collect *frequency data* by tallying how many times that behavior occurs. Examples of frequency data include counting the number of times a child requests a break from work during a session, the number of times that an adult with autism hits himself, the number of times an adolescent makes a conversational initiation to a peer, and the number of times a child asks to use the restroom. An advantage of frequency data is that it is the most common sense way to measure behavior—you merely count how many times it happens. The disadvantage of frequency data is that it can be difficult to collect accurately if the behavior happens at a high rate, if the behavior does not have a clear beginning or end, or if the technician collecting data is also responsible for many other duties at the same time.

Sample Behaviors Measured With Frequency/Rate Recording:

- Raising hand in class
- Asking for desired items
- Biting nails
- Hitting caretaker

Rate. Sometimes when you collect data on a learner's behavior, the amount of time that you observe and collect data might change from one day or session to the next. If you merely look at the frequency of the behavior across these different time periods, it might look like the behavior is happening more or less, when actually it is just because you observed for longer or shorter and therefore had more or less opportunity to see the behavior. For example, if you observed for 1 hour on Monday and you recorded five instances of hitting and then you observed again on Tuesday for 2 hours and again observed five instances of hitting, and you only graph the raw frequency data, then you might believe the behavior was occurring the same amount on both days. In reality, the behavior occurred at double the rate on Monday as it did on Tuesday. If those same frequency data are instead converted into rate, then this difference would be clear (i.e., 5 per hour on Monday vs 2.5 per hour on Tuesday). Frequency data can be converted into frequency per minute, frequency per hour, frequency per day, or frequency per month, depending on what time scale the BCBA wishes to evaluate. In order to *convert frequency data to rate*, you simply divide the total frequency recorded during an observation by the duration of that observation. Fig. 3.1 displays a sample datasheet with

Client: John Doe   Date: January 1st, 2016 Setting: Home

Technician: Sally Smith Session Start: 4:00 pm Session End: 6:00 pm

Behavior	Frequency	Conversion
Aggression	~~卌~~ ///	8 aggression / 2 h = 4 aggression per hour
Tantrums	///	3 tantrums / 2 h = 1.5 tantrums per hour
Mands for attention	~~卌~~ ~~卌~~	10 mands / 2 h = 5 mands per hour
Mands for break	~~卌~~	5 mands / 2 h = 2.5 mands per hour

Figure 3.1 Sample datasheet with frequency data converted to hourly rate.

hypothetical frequency data for various behaviors and demonstrates how they were converted to rate.

3.2.2 Duration

Duration recording is another way of directly measuring a behavior as it occurs in real time. To record *duration* data, note the moment at which the behavior begins and the moment at which the behavior ends, thereby recording the total duration of time that the behavior occurred. This can be done with a stopwatch, timer, or a computerized data collection app. Each time the behavior occurs these measurements are taken. The data for a whole session are then recorded in a logbook or spreadsheet by totaling the total duration of time the behavior occurred during that session. If sessions have different durations, then the total duration of behavior for a session can be divided by the total duration of that session and multiplied by 100, yielding a *percent duration* for that session. For example if a session was 100 minutes long and a child engaged in tantrums for a total of 10 minutes out of that 100 minutes, then the percentage of that session would be 10% duration for tantrums. Fig. 3.2 shows how these hypothetical data were collected. *Average duration* can also be calculated by adding up the total duration and dividing it by the number of occurrences of the behavior.

Depending on how you record duration data, you may also be automatically recording the frequency of that behavior, since you are recording the beginning and end of each occurrence of that behavior. Duration data can be preferable over frequency data alone when the

Client: Jane Smith   Date: January 1st, 2016 Setting: Home

Technician: Jim Doe   Session Start: 12:00 pm Session End: 3:00 pm

Behavior	Duration of Each Occurrence	Total Duration	Percentage of Session
Tantrums			
	60 s	600 s =	10 min / 100 min
	120 s	10 min	= .1
	90 s		
	217 s		.1 x 100 = 10% of session
	113 s		

Figure 3.2 Sample datasheet with duration data converted to percentage of session.

duration of the behavior changes significantly from one occurrence to another. For example, if on Monday Johnny has five tantrums that are each 1 minute in duration and then on Tuesday he has five tantrums that are each 10 minutes in duration, and you only recorded frequency data, then the frequency would appear to be the same on both days, when in reality, the total amount of time spent in tantrums was 10 times more on Tuesday. The disadvantage of duration data is that it can be a burden to collect because it requires the technician to do something at the beginning and end of each instance of behavior.

Sample Behaviors Measured With Duration Recording:
- How long tantrums last
- Length of social play during recess
- How long it takes a child to get dressed

3.2.3 Percentage
Many important skills for individuals with autism have discrete opportunities to occur. For example, when teaching a child her name, the behavior technician might ask the child, "What is your name?," to which the child might respond correctly (e.g., "Martha") or incorrectly (e.g., any response other than "Martha"). When initially teaching this skill, the rate of this response and the duration of this response are not usually what matter the most. The most important dimension of the behavior is the accuracy, so you would most often measure whether the learner responded correctly or incorrectly, each time the behavior technician asked the child her name (later, you may very well want to know that she can respond quickly, too). The total number of correct responses would then be divided by the total number of times the question was asked, and then multiplied by 100, to yield a percentage of correct responding. For example, if the behavior technician asked Martha what her name was 10 different times throughout the session and Martha responded correctly on seven of those occasions, then Martha's percentage correct for that skill would be 70% for that session. Fig. 3.3 shows a sample datasheet with these hypothetical data. Each opportunity or trial for the learner to respond is one row on the datasheet. The first column contains a blank space to write down the specific target you are working on for that trial. In this sample datasheet, the technician worked on the same target ("Martha") for all

trials, so she wrote "Martha" once and then drew an arrow down to save time. The second column contains a code to record the learner's response on each trial (C, correct; I, incorrect; FP, full prompt; PP, partial prompt). The technician circles whichever code corresponds to the learner's response for each trial. The third column contains a code for what prompt, if any, the technician used on that trial (Ph, physical; G, gestural; M, model). The fourth column contains a blank space to write in a different prompt or to record any other relevant notes.

First trial data. Rather than collecting data on all learning trials to yield an overall percentage, some BCBAs prefer to collect data on the accuracy of the first opportunity or trial that a skill is tested each day. This does not mean fewer learning trials are being presented, just that only the learner's first response is tracked. For example, if teaching a child with autism spectrum disorder to respond to the prepositions "on" and "under," you might hand her a ball and deliver the instruction "Put on" or "Put under" on alternating trials. For standard percentage data, you would record the accuracy of every trial of both targets all day and then average the percentage correct for each target at the end of each session or day. To collect first trial data, you would record only the accuracy of the very first trial of the day that each

Client: Martha Doe   Date: January 1st, 2016 Setting: Home

Technician: Sally Smith Program: Social Identification Questions

Instruction: "What is your name?"   Response: "Martha"

Trial	Target	Response			Prompt (if any)			Notes
1	Martha	C ⓘ	FP	PP	Ph	G	M	
2		Ⓒ I	FP	PP	Ph	G	M	
3		Ⓒ I	FP	PP	Ph	G	M	
4		Ⓒ I	FP	PP	Ph	G	M	
5		Ⓒ I	FP	PP	Ph	G	M	
6		C ⓘ	FP	PP	Ph	G	M	
7		C I	FP	ⓅⓅ	Ph	G	Ⓜ	"Mah…"
8		Ⓒ I	FP	PP	Ph	G	M	
9		Ⓒ I	FP	PP	Ph	G	M	
10		Ⓒ I	FP	PP	Ph	G	M	
Summary: 7 / 10 x 100 = 70%								

Figure 3.3 Sample percentage datasheet.

target ("on" and "under") was taught. Proponents of first trial data collection suggest that you may be able to present even more learning opportunities as less time is spent collecting data. Emerging research suggests that data collected for every trial of learning and first trial data collection may be equally accurate.

It is worth noting that every organization and school uses somewhat different datasheets and there is no right or wrong way. It is important to check with your supervising BCBA to make sure you are collecting data in the manner specified, so that the learner's data are consistent across technicians.

Sample Behaviors Measured With Percentage Recording:

- Response to instructions
- Responding to others' greetings
- Percentage of bites consumed

3.2.4 Latency

Sometimes it is important for a learner with autism to do a skill quickly. For example, many social and conversational skills only work if they are done fast. For instance, if a peer approaches a child with autism and asks their name, and the child takes 10 seconds to answer, the peer will likely have already walked away, perhaps thinking the child with autism was intentionally ignoring them. Latency recording is used to measure how quickly or slowly a behavior occurred after an opportunity began. To measure *latency*, use a stopwatch or an electronic data collection app to measure the time from the onset of an opportunity to respond, to the beginning of the learner's response. Latency data are usually then summarized by totaling all latencies recorded and then dividing that total by the number of latencies recorded, thus yielding an average latency for that session.

Sample Behaviors Measured With Latency Recording:

- Time from instruction to begin getting dressed
- Time from instruction to begin tabletop work
- Time lapsed from peer asking favorite movie to response
- Time lapsed from work beginning to onset of aggression

3.2.5 Discontinuous Measurement

Discontinuous measurement is usually considered less valid than continuous measurement because *discontinuous measurement* does not record all of the behavior as it actually occurs during an observation, but rather, records some estimate of the occurrence of the behavior during that observation. Discontinuous measurement is usually used when continuous measurement of rate or duration would be too difficult for you to do, given all of the other demands placed on you in the moment (e.g., recording other behaviors, teaching multiple skills, etc.). Below, we describe how to record partial interval data, whole interval data, and momentary time sampling.

3.2.6 Partial Interval

Partial interval is probably the most commonly used type of discontinuous measurement. *Partial interval* data collection involves recording the presence or absence of a behavior during many consecutive brief intervals of time. Each observation is divided into many equal consecutive intervals of a particular amount of time. For example, if you are going to collect data for 10 minutes you might divide those 10 minutes into twenty 30-second intervals. You would then record whether or not the behavior occurred at all during each of those intervals. If the behavior occurs even for a moment during a particular interval then you score a plus (by writing a plus or circling a plus on the datasheet) for that interval. If the behavior did not occur at all during that interval then you would score a minus (by writing a minus or circling a minus on the datasheet). You then summarize the data for that observation by tallying the total number of intervals in which the behavior occurred at all and then divide that number by the total number of intervals you observed and then multiply the resulting decimal by 100, yielding a percentage of the observation in which the behavior was observed. Fig. 3.4 displays a sample interval datasheet with 20 intervals. Note that there is no correct or incorrect number of intervals or duration of each interval for an interval datasheet. Also, note that the same interval datasheet can be used for partial interval, whole interval, or momentary time sampling (see whole interval and momentary time sampling below).

A significant advantage of partial interval data collection is that it does not always require the data collector to give her undivided attention to observing the behavior for the entire duration of every interval

Client: Martha Doe   Date: January 1st, 2016 Setting: Home

Technician: Sally Smith Target Behavior: Vocal Stereotypy

Partial Interval Data

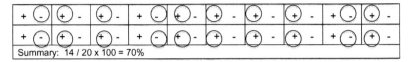

Summary: 14 / 20 x 100 = 70%

Whole Interval Data

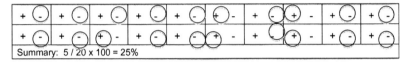

Summary: 5 / 20 x 100 = 25%

Momentary Time Sampling

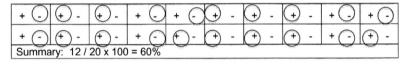

Summary: 12 / 20 x 100 = 60%

Figure 3.4 Sample interval datasheets with 20 intervals each. From top to bottom, the three sample datasheets depict hypothetical partial interval, whole interval, and momentary time sampling data for the same observation.

because, if the behavior occurs at all then you would score a plus, and then there is no need to observe that behavior for the remainder of that interval. For this reason, partial interval data collection can sometimes be less cumbersome than frequency data. Another major advantage of partial interval data is that it can be used to collect data on behaviors which do not have a clear beginning and end, e.g., behaviors that start and stop frequently, so it might be difficult to determine when it counts as a new occurrence if you were taking frequency data. In addition, partial interval data can be useful for collecting data on behaviors that change in their duration from time to time, where you would normally like to take duration data, if you could. For example, if crying occurs for 30 seconds sometimes and for up to 5 minutes at other times, then a mere frequency count would fail to represent that accurately. Partial interval data would provide an estimate of the overall duration by providing an indication of the number of intervals it occurred in.

Like all procedures, partial interval data collection has its limitations. Perhaps the greatest limitation is that it is discontinuous, so it is inevitably a rough estimate. Recall that if the behavior occurs for only one instant in an interval, the entire interval would still be scored with a plus. So if you had an interval of 30 seconds and the behavior occurred for 1 second it would be scored in the same way as if the behavior occurred for all 30 seconds. Therefore partial interval data tend to overestimate the actual occurrence of the behavior. For this reason it is generally considered best practice to use partial interval data as a measure for behaviors you are attempting to reduce because the potential overestimate will lead to a more conservative estimate about treatment effect. In other words, if you are trying to decrease a behavior and your data tell you that the behavior is a bit worse than it actually is, that will encourage the team to continue working hard on that behavior and not falsely influence you to believe you are making more progress than you really are.

One thing to consider when using partial interval data collection is that the duration of the intervals will affect the accuracy of the data greatly. Generally speaking, the shorter the intervals, the more accurate the data will be, and the longer the intervals, the less accurate the data will be but the easier it will be to collect the data. For example, imagine the difference between two extremes: 1 second intervals, which would be very close to continuous measurement of the behavior, compared to 1 hour intervals, which would be such a crude estimate of behavior that it would be almost useless. At the same time, something that needs to be balanced against the concern for accuracy is the need for a data collection system that is practical for the behavior technician to use. The BCBA supervising the treatment team will need to balance the need for accurate data with the need for easy data collection for the technicians, and find the most reasonable compromise that still provides an accurate estimate of the overall occurrence of the behavior.

Sample Behaviors Measured With Partial Interval Recording:

- Hand flapping during recess
- Vocal stereotypy during free play
- Biting finger nails

3.2.7 Whole Interval

Whole interval data collection is often considered the flipside of partial interval data. To collect *whole interval* data, you record a plus for each interval in which the behavior occurred for the entire duration of the interval. For example, to measure on-task behavior, you could observe a student and record every 30-second interval during which the student has his eyes oriented toward his work for the entire 30-second interval. The second panel of Fig. 3.4 depicts sample whole interval data.

Whole interval data collection also has its own strengths and limitations. One strength is that, since the behavior often does not occur for the entire duration of any particular interval, the observer will often not need to observe the entire interval. For example, if a learner engages in the behavior for the first 35 seconds of a 1 minute interval but then stops, then you would not need to observe that behavior during the remaining 25 seconds of that interval because you already know that interval will be recorded as a minus.

One thing to consider is that whole interval data collection generally underestimates the behavior. Note, this is the opposite of partial interval data. Because the behavior need only be absent for 1 second in an interval and that behavior would still be scored as a minus for that entire interval, it is likely that the behavior will be underestimated. For example, if you were scoring a child's social engagement while playing with peers during 10 second intervals, and she stopped engaging socially for only 1 second out of a 10 second interval, that interval would still be scored as a minus even though the behavior actually occurred 90% of the time during that interval. Just like it is wise to use partial interval data only for behaviors you want to decrease, it is wise to use whole interval data only for behaviors you want to increase so that any amount of underestimation of the appearance of the behavior will result in a more conservative estimate of the effectiveness of your intervention.

Sample Behaviors Measured With Whole Interval Recording:

- Cooperative play during recess
- Toy engagement during free play
- Task engagement with worksheets

3.2.8 Momentary Time Sampling

Momentary time sampling data collection involves recording whether or not the behavior occurred right at the moment the interval elapsed. For example, if you were collecting data on vocal stereotypy in a learner with autism across continuous 5 minute intervals, you would observe the behavior at the moment each 5 minute interval elapsed and record a plus or minus for that moment only, regardless of what occurred over the previous 5 minutes. Momentary time sampling data enjoys one major advantage over virtually all other data collection systems, i.e., that you are not required to observe the behavior for the vast majority of session time. For this reason, momentary time sampling is a preferred method of data collection in many situations in which the technician is already very busy with other tasks such as teaching and collecting data. For example, while it would likely be unreasonable to ask a classroom teacher who was busy with 20 students to collect continuous data on individual students, it might be reasonable to establish a momentary time sampling data collection procedure with a few particular students and behaviors, with reasonably long interval duration. The bottom of Fig. 3.4 displays hypothetical momentary time sampling data.

Sample Behaviors Measured With Momentary Time Sampling Recording:

• Social engagement during recess for several students
• Attending to book for multiple kids during story time
• Vocal stereotypy during free play

3.3 OTHER DATA COLLECTION METHODS

3.3.1 Permanent Product Recording

Permanent product recording is different from other data collection procedures because it does not involve measuring the actual behavior. Instead, to record *permanent product* data, you measure some physical product that the behavior produced. For example, when measuring the accuracy of a student's work on a worksheet, you could grade the written answers on the worksheet some time after the student completed it. A major advantage of permanent product recording is that it requires zero direct observation of the behavior. Instead, you record at a later time when it is convenient for you to measure the permanent product.

A major disadvantage to never directly observing the behavior is that the permanent product may not be an accurate measurement. For example, if you do not observe the student completing the worksheet, it is possible that someone else completed the worksheet, the student cheated, or relied on assistance from parents or others.

Sample Behaviors Measured With Permanent Product Recording:

- Completing homework
- Washing the dog
- Cleaning the bathroom
- Constructing bracelets
- Ripping paper
- Breaking items

3.4 SUMMARIZING AND GRAPHING DATA

Recording accurate data is critical, but it is meaningless if the data are not entered, summarized, and graphed so that they can be analyzed for the purpose of evaluating treatment. Your BCBA will have specified how she wants the data to be entered and summarized for each learner that you work with. Generally speaking, data can be graphed by hand onto a paper graph or can be entered into an electronic spreadsheet, such as with Microsoft Excel. One of the advantages of electronic data collection is that some programs can be configured to automatically enter data into relevant spreadsheets and generate computerized graphs of data.

Frequency data are usually summarized as the rate for each session or day. Duration data can be summarized as the total duration for a given session or that total duration can be divided by the entire duration of a session, and multiplied by 100, thereby yielding a percentage of the session during which the behavior occurred. Partial interval, whole interval, and momentary time sampling data are summarized as the percentage of intervals during which the behavior was recorded.

You should summarize and enter data how your BCBA designates, generally at the end of every session or every day. Once the data are summarized, you should graph them according to your BCBA's directions. Data should usually be graphed after every session, observation, or block of trials.

Graphing Guidelines

- Label the horizontal axis with sessions or days, as specified by your BCBA
- Label the vertical axis with the type of measurement you are using (e.g., percent correct, percentage of session, hourly rate, daily rate, etc.)
- Graph one data point for every session or block of trials
- Draw a solid line connecting data points in the same phase
- Draw a vertical phase line to separate phases of treatment
- Do not connect data points between different phases
- Label the phase at the top of the phase (e.g., baseline, treatment, etc.)
- Use different symbols to depict different behaviors on the same graph
- Use a legend or written names with arrows to label the different behaviors if more than one behavior is depicted on the same graph

The reason the data should be graphed frequently is so that the team can analyze the learner's progress and make decisions about what, if anything, about the behavior reduction or skill acquisition program should be adjusted.

Fig. 3.5 depicts sample challenging behavior data graphed, with a target behavior (tantrums) and a replacement behavior (communication) graphed on the same graph. Note the graph starts with a baseline phase, where data were collected for several days before the behavior reduction plan began. After the treatment phase began, indicated by

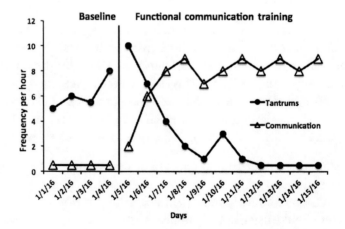

Figure 3.5 Sample graph of challenging behavior and communication in baseline and treatment phases.

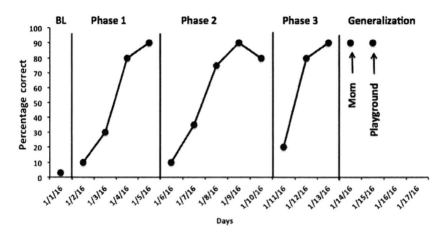

Figure 3.6 Sample skill acquisition graph.

the vertical phase line, tantrums gradually reduced and communication gradually increased.

Fig. 3.6 depicts sample data from a skill acquisition program, teaching a learner with autism to identify others' emotions. Note the graph begins with a short baseline probe to ensure the learner does not already have the skill. The graph depicts the percentage of trials in which the learner makes a correct response. Note that the accuracy of the learner's responses gradually increases. Each skill acquisition program is different but this hypothetical program has three phases. When each new phase is introduced, accuracy decreases and gradually increases until it is consistently high, at which point the next phase is introduced. Note that after phase 3 is mastered, data are collected on generalization across people and settings (see Section 5.13).

CHAPTER 4

Assessment

In this chapter, we teach you about the various methods of assessment that are used in ABA treatment for individuals with autism spectrum disorder and how you, as a behavior technician, will help with them. Assessment may be less interesting than treatment but it is equally critical. Without assessment, there is no way for the team to know what to treat. Assessment provides a starting point and road map to steer the treatment team in the right direction.

4.1 OBSERVABLE AND MEASURABLE DESCRIPTIONS OF BEHAVIOR AND ENVIRONMENT

In Chapter 3, Measurement and Data Collection, we described how to measure behavior. However, before you can use any of those methods effectively, you have to know exactly what behavior you are measuring, so you can be sure of what constitutes a response and what does not. *Operational definitions* are definitions of behavior that tell you what behaviors to observe and exactly which individual occurrences should be recorded. Good operational definitions should be:

- *Objective.* Operational definitions only include directly observable aspects of behavior (e.g., hitting), not unobservable internal states (e.g., frustration).
- *Clear.* Operational definitions should be unambiguous. Anyone, without any prior knowledge of the behavior, should be able to understand the definition. A good test is that a person who has never seen the behavior can "act it out" from the definition.
- *Complete.* The definition includes all of the information necessary for you to discriminate between the behavior and other behaviors that are similar but do not count. Including specific examples and nonexamples is often helpful.
- *Individualized.* The particular forms of a behavior that one individual displays will likely be different from those of another. For

Training Manual for Behavior Technicians Working with Individuals with Autism.
DOI: http://dx.doi.org/10.1016/B978-0-12-809408-2.00004-0

Table 4.1 Examples of Stronger and Weaker Operational Definitions. Try to Identify How the Weaker Ones Are Less Objective, Clear, and/or Complete

Behavior	Weaker Definition	Stronger Definition
Tantrum	Acting out by showing frustration and crying	Screaming or crying, lasting longer than 3 s, with or without throwing self on floor, excluding whining at or below a conversational volume
Aggression	Physical assault with intent to do harm	Hitting, kicking, biting, or slapping
Interactive play	Having fun with others	Responding in a socially appropriate and on-topic manner in the context of play, within 3 s of a peer making a play initiation
Functional pretend play	Appropriate toy play	Interacting with a toy in a manner in which it is intended by the manufacturer. Examples include making a truck drive, making a doll eat, and pretending to drink tea from a tea cup. Nonexamples include interacting with toys in stereotyped or repetitive ways, such as turning a truck upside down and spinning the wheels, repeatedly twirling a doll in circles, or repeatedly staring at a tea cup out of the corner of one's eyes

example, Jimmy's aggression might include hitting and kicking, whereas Sally's might include pinching and scratching.

Table 4.1 displays sample operational definitions. The middle column has operational definitions that are weaker and the right column has ones that are stronger. See if you can identify what about the weaker definitions is less objective, less clear, and/or less complete.

It is often necessary to operationally define events that occur in the environment. For example, when collecting functional assessment data (see below), you will record what happens in the learner's environment immediately before and after challenging behavior occurs. Definitions of environmental events should also be objective, clear, and complete.

4.1.1 Preference Assessments

Preference assessments are procedures that you conduct to help you predict what consequences you can deliver to the learner that are likely to work as reinforcers. Since reinforcement is the single most important part of being an effective behavior technician, preference assessments are quite crucial. A variety of preference assessment procedures have been shown to be effective in research. Although professionals and family members usually believe they know what a learner likes the most, plenty of research has shown that when you give the learner the opportunity to show you what they want, that is a much better indication of what will actually work as a reinforcer than if you ask family and staff.

4.1.2 Identifying the Items to Include in the Preference Assessment

A preference assessment is only as good as the items that you pick to include in it, so you need to ensure that you pick a variety of items that the learner likes. To do this, ask knowledgeable caregivers (e.g., the learner herself, family members, teachers, staff, etc.). Identify 6−12 items that satisfy a variety of senses (i.e., things the learner would like to see, hear, touch, and so on). If you want to include edible items, then consider conducting separate assessments for edible versus nonedible items because sometimes an individual will pick only edible items, even if nonedible items are also powerful reinforcers.

4.1.3 Single Item Preference Assessment

The single item preference assessment was the first preference assessment developed and it is the simplest. To do it, simply present one item at a time to the learner and record whether he consumes/interacts with it, makes no response to it, or avoids it (e.g., cries, throws it, etc.). For edible items, present a small piece or one bite of the item. For nonedible items, allow the learner to interact with the item for 30 seconds and then present the next trial. Present all the items on your list in a random order. Present each item three times total. Tally the number of times each item was consumed/interacted with. Fig. 4.1 is a sample datasheet you can use for the assessment. The items that were consumed/interacted with the most are more likely to be effective reinforcers than the other items.

4.1.4 Paired Choice Preference Assessment

One problem with the single item preference assessment is that a learner may consume/interact with all items (especially if none are non-preferred), in which case you will not be able to identify which items are more highly preferred than others. The paired choice procedure was developed to address this problem because it requires that the learner make choices between items and therefore reliably produces a hierarchy of preference for items.

To conduct a paired choice assessment, you first need to designate how you are going to pair each item with every other item once.

Learner: Date: Assessor:

Item 1:_____   Item 2:_____   Item 3:_____
Item 4:_____   Item 5:_____   Item 6:_____
Item 7:_____   Item 8:_____   Item 9:_____

Data: Consumed / Interacted with = C   Avoid = A   No response: NR

Instructions:
- Present all items, one at a time, in the order specified below
- Circle the data code that corresponds with the learner's response each time an item is presented
- Allow the learner to consume one bite/interact with the item for 30 seconds then remove it and present the next item

Item	Response			Item	Response			Item	Response		
1	C	A	NR	3	C	A	NR	9	C	A	NR
2	C	A	NR	8	C	A	NR	8	C	A	NR
3	C	A	NR	7	C	A	NR	7	C	A	NR
4	C	A	NR	4	C	A	NR	6	C	A	NR
5	C	A	NR	9	C	A	NR	5	C	A	NR
6	C	A	NR	6	C	A	NR	4	C	A	NR
7	C	A	NR	1	C	A	NR	3	C	A	NR
8	C	A	NR	2	C	A	NR	2	C	A	NR
9	C	A	NR	5	C	A	NR	1	C	A	NR

Figure 4.1 Sample single item preference assessment datasheet.

Learner: Date: Assessor:

Item 1:_____ Item 2:_____ Item 3:_____ Item 4:_____

Item 5:_____ Item 6:_____ Item 7:_____

Instructions:
- Present the items in pairs, in the sequence of pairs specified below.
- Circle the number corresponding to the item that the learner consumed/interacted with
- If the learner avoids an item, write an A over the number that corresponds to that item
- If a learner does not choose either item, write "no response" for that trial
- Summarize the data according to the percentage of trials each item was chosen
- Items chosen the most are likely to be the strongest reinforcers

1	2	3	5	2	5
3	7	4	6	1	6
5	6	1	5	2	4
2	3	2	7	3	6
4	5	3	4	1	7
6	7	5	7	2	6
1	3	1	4	4	7

Figure 4.2 Sample paired choice preference assessment datasheet.

You can randomly pair items yourself or you can use Fig. 4.2, which is a datasheet that has prerandomized all the pairings you need for an assessment that includes up to seven items. All you need to do is randomly decide which item is item one, two, etc. For each pair that you present, allow the learner to only choose one. If she reaches for more than one, take both items away and represent the trial. For each trial, record the one item that the learner consumes/interacts with. If the learner does not respond or refuses both items, record that, and present the next trial.

If you are including a large number of items in your paired choice assessment, you may need to schedule more than one session to finish the assessment. When all trials have been presented, tally the number of times each item was chosen and consumed/interacted with, divide that by the total number of opportunities the learner had to choose it, and multiply that by 100, giving you a percentage of times each item was chosen. Items with higher percentages are more likely to be effective reinforcers than items that were chosen less.

4.1.5 Multiple Stimulus Preference Assessment
One major disadvantage of the paired choice assessment is the time that it takes to implement and therefore it is not likely to be done very frequently in daily practice. The multiple stimulus preference assessment is a procedure that can be conducted much more quickly and can therefore be a good choice for learners who have the ability to scan multiple items before making a choice. The multiple stimulus procedure should usually only be conducted with between three and seven items (more than seven may require too much scanning for many learners).

Fig. 4.3 is a sample datasheet for a multiple stimulus preference assessment with up to seven items. To conduct the multiple stimulus procedure, place all items in a line on a table in front of the learner and ask her to choose one. If she tries to choose more than one at a time, block access to all items and re-present the trial. When the learner picks an item, record which item was chosen and allow her to consume it/interact with it for 30 seconds. Then represent the remaining items and allow the learner to choose again. Repeat this process until no items remain. Summarize the data by ordering the items in terms of the sequence in which they were chosen. Items chosen earlier

Learner: Date: Assessor:

Item 1:_____   Item 2:_____   Item 3:_____
Item 4:_____   Item 5:_____   Item 6:_____
Item 7:_____

Instructions:
- Present an array of items and only allow the learner to choose one item
- Allow the learner to consume the item she chooses (if edible) or interact with it for 30 seconds
- When the learner makes a choice, remove the unchosen items and represent only the remaining unchosen items on the next trial.
- Record the item that the learner chose and consumed/interacted with on each trial
- Repeat the entire assessment once or twice and summarize data across all repetitions to increase validity
- Items chosen earlier are more likely to be effective reinforcers than items chosen later

Trial	Item Chosen	Notes
1		
2		
3		
4		
5		
6		
7		

Figure 4.3 Sample multiple stimulus preference assessment datasheet.

are likely to be effective reinforcers. To make the results more reliable, repeat it once or twice and average the data.

The procedure described above is called the *Multiple Stimulus Without Replacement (MSWO) Preference Assessment* because, after the learner chooses an item, that item is *not* replaced in the array of items when presenting the next trial. A variation of the procedure is called the *Multiple Stimulus With Replacement (MSW) Preference Assessment* because the item that a learner chooses *is* replaced when presenting the next trial. The *MSWO* is by far the more commonly used variation.

4.1.6 Frequent Brief Multiple Stimulus Assessments

A common and very practical way to implement preference assessments throughout the day is to conduct one-trial multiple stimulus assessments before each new program, lesson, or activity, or any time you believe the learner's motivation is lagging (decreasing attention, slower at responding to instructions, etc.). To implement frequent brief multiple stimulus assessments, simply present two or three items and ask the learner to select one. Whichever item the learner selects is the reinforcer that you will use during instruction until the next brief multiple stimulus assessment is conducted or until the learner independently asks to earn a different reinforcer. Conducting these assessments about once every 10 minutes or so ensures that your reinforcement procedures are sensitive to what the learner prefers in the moment. Data from these frequent one-trial assessments can be averaged across the day to summarize relative preference between the many items assessed, across the day.

Remember: Something is only a reinforcer if it increases behavior. Take cues from the learner. If the learner is no longer actively engaged in what you are teaching, pause to conduct a brief preference assessment. You need to have effective reinforcers in order to teach new skills.

4.2 SKILL ACQUISITION ASSESSMENT PROCEDURES

Your supervising BCBA may ask you to collect data on skills, according to a variety of skill acquisition assessments. Popular examples include the *Verbal Behavior Milestones Assessment and Placement Program* (VB-MAPP: Sundberg, 2008), the *Assessment of Basic Language and Learning Skills—Revised* (ABLLS-R: Partington, 2008), and the *PEAK: Relational Training System* (Dixon, 2015). To collect data for skill acquisition assessments, your BCBA will specify exactly what instructions to give or environmental arrangements to set up and which behaviors to record the presence of, absence of, or rate of. For example, when assessing manding (i.e., requesting), you might withhold a learner's favorite toy and look "expectantly" at the learner and wait 5 seconds. If the learner requests the toy by stating its name, you might record that the learner responded correctly and then give the toy to the learner. Other skill acquisition assessments might require that you merely observe the learner, without asking her to do anything, and simply record data on her behavior. For example, you might observe a 5 year-old girl playing with her sibling and record the frequency of spontaneous verbal initiations she makes to her sibling.

The particular skill acquisition assessment procedures you will conduct will be completely different for each learner and for each skill being assessed. Generally speaking, you do not provide prompts or cues during skill acquisition assessments. In addition, some skill acquisition procedures require that you do not provide any consequences (e.g., reinforcement or error correction) to the learner because you are looking for a pure test of what the learner can do, without any support from others.

4.2.1 Baseline/Probing

Before beginning to teach a new skill, a brief baseline or probe should be conducted in order to identify whether the learner already has the skill. To baseline a skill, present the instruction without a prompt and record the learner's response. Some agencies and schools reinforce correct responses during baseline and some do not. The rationale for reinforcing during baseline is that you want to encourage correct responding—you do not want to put it on extinction! But the rationale for not reinforcing correct responding during baseline is that it could influence how accurate the learner is going to be throughout baseline and therefore will give you a less pure test of the learner's ability. For an analogy, consider the fact that you never receive feedback on answers in the middle of an exam in school. The pros and cons of both sides are legitimate and the decision needs to be made on a case-by-case basis for each learner, so follow your BCBA's instructions. In addition, various agencies and schools differ in terms of the length and extent of baseline that they conduct. The minimum is a single trial or probe of a skill. All other things being equal, the more trials you conduct, the more accurate baseline you will get, but the more time you take away from teaching and the more you run the risk of evoking problem behavior by allowing the learner to fail repeatedly and not giving help in the form of prompting. Again, follow your supervising BCBA's guidelines.

4.3 FUNCTIONAL ASSESSMENT PROCEDURES

Functional assessments are procedures that help the team discover why a learner engages in a particular challenging behavior. Functional assessments are designed and supervised by your supervising BCBA, but as a behavior technician you will have the opportunity to help with several aspects of the process, as we describe below.

4.3.1 Antecedent-Behavior-Consequence Data

In order to discover why a learner displays challenging behavior, the team will want to identify what ongoing sources of reinforcement the behavior is receiving in the learner's daily life (see Section 6.1.7).

Recording *antecedents*, what happens in the environment immediately before a behavior, and recording *consequences*, what happens in the environment immediately after a behavior, is called *Antecedent-Behavior-Consequence (ABC) Recording*. ABC recording helps the BCBA figure out what effect the behavior has on the environment because it reveals how the behavior changes the environment. For example, if the learner is being asked to do something difficult (A) and he hits his parent (B) and then the parent gives him a break to calm him down (C), then the behavior had the effect of eliminating the task. In this case, the antecedent was a demand, the behavior was hitting, and the consequence was removal of the demand (a break).

You will learn more about common functions of behavior in Chapter 6, Behavior Reduction, but for now, it will suffice to say that the most common antecedents you will look for and record are *low attention, denied access to preferred item or activity*, or the presence of a *demand*. The most common consequences you will look for and record are someone giving the learner *attention*, getting *access to a preferred item or activity* (or not having to share or give it up), and *escape* from/reduction/postponement of a demand. There are a large variety of ways to collect data on these antecedents and consequences, but most of them can be described as either narrative or structured. For all ABC data, you want to directly observe the learner in the various settings in the natural environment where the challenging behavior usually occurs.

Narrative ABC data. To record narrative ABC data, you watch the learner and every time the target challenging behavior occurs, you write that down, as well as writing down what happened immediately before and after (i.e., the immediate antecedents and consequences). Remember to only write down what you can directly observe (e.g., the teacher asked Jimmy to do his worksheet), not inferences (e.g., Jimmy was bored). If you want to record data that indicate the learner's internal states (e.g., Jimmy didn't want to do his work), just describe what you saw and heard that made you think he had that internal state (e.g., Jimmy said "I don't want to do my work"). Fig. 4.4 is a sample narrative ABC datasheet filled out for a hypothetical learner. After a substantial number of antecedents, behaviors, and consequences have occurred, your supervising BCBA will summarize the data and analyze it according to what behavioral functions it suggests.

Antecedents	Behaviors	Consequences
Mom asked Jimmy to pick up his dirty clothes	Jimmy screamed and fell to the floor	Mom told Jimmy he could clean up his clothes later
Dad asked Jimmy to take a bath	Jimmy bit dad	Dad told him "No!" and gave Jimmy five minutes to calm down before bath
Brother asked Jimmy to share the computer	Jimmy screamed and shoved brother	Brother cried and walked away

Figure 4.4 Sample narrative ABC datasheet.

Client: **Date:**   **Assessor:**   **Setting:**

Behavior 1:_____ **Behavior 2:**_____ **Behavior 3:**_____

Antecedent codes: LA = low attention, RA = restricted access to preferred item / activity, D = demand given, N = None of the above

Consequence codes: A = attention given, AG = access granted, B = Break given / demand lessened / postponed, N = None of the above

Instructions:
- Each time one of the target behaviors occur, circle the number that corresponds with that behavior in the center column and circle all of the antecedent and consequence codes that apply, in the left and right column
- Write descriptive notes of any events that the codes do not capture at the bottom or in the margins of the data sheet

Antecedents				Behaviors			Consequences			
LA	RA	D	N	1	2	3	A	AG	B	N
LA	RA	D	N	1	2	3	A	AG	B	N
LA	RA	D	N	1	2	3	A	AG	B	N
LA	RA	D	N	1	2	3	A	AG	B	N
LA	RA	D	N	1	2	3	A	AG	B	N
LA	RA	D	N	1	2	3	A	AG	B	N
LA	RA	D	N	1	2	3	A	AG	B	N
LA	RA	D	N	1	2	3	A	AG	B	N

Figure 4.5 Sample structured ABC datasheet.

Structured ABC data. To record structured ABC data, your supervising BCBA will provide you with a datasheet that has specific categories of antecedents, behaviors, and consequences. Each time a target challenging behavior occurs, you indicate with circling or check marks which antecedents, behaviors, and consequences occurred. Keep in mind that often more than one antecedent or consequence may occur and check all that apply. For example, imagine a teacher who asked a learner to complete his work, the learner then screamed, and the teacher then reprimanded him and sent him to timeout. The antecedent would be recorded as a demand but the consequences include both attention (i.e., the reprimand) and escape (i.e., he was not required to do his work in timeout). Fig. 4.5 is a sample structured ABC datasheet.

Be extra careful to pay enough attention to notice all of the things that are happening in the learner's environment immediately before the behavior and all of the changes that the learner's behavior produced in the environment (e.g., gets more attention, gets escape from work, gets access to a preferred item). The most common mistake that behavior technicians make during ABC data collection is writing down inferences that refer to things that aren't actually observable (e.g., inner states, events from the past, etc.). Make sure to only record what you actually see and hear.

CHAPTER 5

Skill Acquisition

Skill acquisition is the part of applied behavior analysis (ABA) treatment that focuses on teaching and maintaining new skills to help the learner function more independently and productively in life. It is by far the most important thing that you will do in working as a behavior technician with learners with autism spectrum disorder (ASD). Even when working with a learner who exhibits severe problem behavior, the most effective way to treat that behavior is not to focus on what the learner should *not do*, but rather to focus on what she *should do*. In addition, many individuals with ASD have deficits in basic communication abilities, so they learn how to use challenging behaviors to get what they want or need. For all of these reasons, focusing on teaching strong communication skills, independent living skills, social skills, and leisure or play skills, is the best way to prevent challenging behavior and to ensure that the learners you work with function as independently as possible.

5.1 ESSENTIAL COMPONENTS OF A WRITTEN SKILL ACQUISITION PLAN

A skill acquisition plan is a written document that specifies how you are going to teach a particular skill to the learner you are working with. It is important to follow the skill acquisition plan carefully and for all behavior technicians working with that learner to implement the plan with high consistency. The reason for this is that, if the plan does not work but it is not being implemented consistently, then the BCBA supervising the case will not be able to determine whether it is the plan that is ineffective or whether it is merely failing due to a lack in treatment integrity with the behavior technicians not implementing it consistently. Below we describe the essential elements that you can expect

Training Manual for Behavior Technicians Working with Individuals with Autism.
DOI: http://dx.doi.org/10.1016/B978-0-12-809408-2.00005-2

Program: Functions of Objects

Terminal Goal: The learner will accurately follow instructions comprised of functions of items by discriminating among stimuli naturally occurring in the environment (finding glue for an art project), will use language to identify items by their functions within requests ("I need a chair to sit") and social comments ("These shoes are good for climbing"), and conversational exchanges ("How do you drive the car fast?").

- Incremental Goal 1 (Listener)
  - ➢ Antecedent/Instruction: *"Which one do you need to (function)?"*
  - ➢ Target Response: *Learner selects needed object for identified function*
- Incremental Goal 2 (Mand)
  - ➢ Antecedent/Instruction: *Learner does not have needed object to carry out function*
  - ➢ Target Response: *Learner requests needed object*
- Incremental Goal 3 (Tact)
  - ➢ Antecedent/Instruction: *Learner sees object*
  - ➢ Target Response: *Learner comments on function of object*
- Incremental Goal 4 (Intraverbal)
  - ➢ Antecedent/Instruction: *"What do you do with (object)?" or "What do you (function) with?"*
  - ➢ Target Response: *"You (function) with (object)"*

Targets to teach:	
Object	Function(s)
Ball	*Throw, kick, catch*
Fork / Spoon / Plate	*Eat*
Cup	*Drink*
Crayon	*Color, draw*
Car	*Drive*

Materials Needed: *Everyday objects from target list*	
Teaching Procedures: *Natural environment training*	
Prompting / Prompt Fading: *Most to least (full verbal model, partial verbal model, delay to verbal model)*	

Figure 5.1 Sample skill acquisition plan for teaching a learner the different functions of everyday objects.

to find in most skill acquisition plans. Fig. 5.1 is a sample of a skill acquisition plan for teaching various functions of everyday objects.

5.1.1 Terminal Skill or Goal

Skill acquisition plans should specify the overall target to be taught. For example, if the objective is to teach social imitation (i.e., a learner spontaneously imitating others within social contexts), then individual target responses such as imitating clapping and waving might be smaller component skills along the way to teaching the generalized repertoire of imitation. The plan may also describe the overall purpose. For example, a plan may be attempting to accomplish the goal of teaching functional pretend play with narration (goal), with the overall rationale of improving the learner's social play skills (purpose).

Purpose-Driven Programming. Keep in mind where you are headed when teaching a skill and be careful to not get lost in the details, it is the big picture that really matters.

5.1.2 Teaching Procedures

Skill acquisition plans should specify what teaching procedures are to be used for that plan. For example, using discrete trial teaching versus natural environment teaching versus chaining. The various procedures you may use are described in detail later in this chapter.

5.1.3 Materials

Skill acquisition plans will likely specify the particular teaching materials you will need to run the program. For example, for a program teaching manding (requesting) to a child with autism, you might need to have his highest preferred toys available. For teaching an adult with ASD how to make a sandwich, you might need to have bread, mayonnaise, mustard, cheese, turkey, a plate, and a knife available. For teaching a child the names of objects, you may need to have several examples of the objects you are teaching.

5.1.4 Preparing the Learning Environment

Generally speaking, you should always minimize distractions and have appropriate reinforcers available. If there are any particular ways in which you need to prepare the environment, the skill acquisition plan should specify these. For example, if you are teaching a child with autism to mand (request) his favorite food, you might place that food in sight but out of reach (e.g., on the kitchen counter or on a shelf). If you are teaching an adolescent to ask for help, you might set up a preferred activity that is incomplete (e.g., a puzzle with a piece missing, iPad with passcode enabled) in order to create an opportunity for her to ask you for help.

Arrange the environment for success to prevent challenging behavior:

- Position yourself between learner and door to prevent elopement
- Clear table of extraneous materials to prevent throwing
- Ready materials prior to calling the listener over to prevent unnecessary waiting and resulting problem behavior

5.1.5 Instruction

The skill acquisition plan should specify what instructions to deliver. For example, when teaching a learner with ASD to make reciprocal conversational statements, the instruction might consist of the behavior technician asking, "Hey, what did you do yesterday?" Or if you are teaching a child his phone number, the instruction might be, "What's your phone number?" Or if you were teaching a child with autism receptive object labels (aka listener behavior) for clothing, the instruction might be, "Which one is the shirt?"

5.1.6 Target Response

The skill acquisition plan will then specify what particular target response(s) you are expecting from the learner. For example, when teaching a child with ASD categories, in response to the instruction, "Tell me some animals," a correct response on the part of the learner might be "Horse, dog, cat," or any other animal. Table 5.1 displays sample instructions and responses for a variety of different skill acquisition programs.

It is important for the skill acquisition plan to clearly define what counts and what does not count as a correct response so all behavior technicians on the team can implement the program consistently. If

Table 5.1 Sample Instructions and Responses		
Program	**Technician Instruction**	**Learner Response**
Social identification: Name	"What's your name?"	"Jimmy"
Features	"Tell me some things that have wings"	"Airplanes, birds, and angels"
Functional pretend play: Responding to initiations	"Let's play with blocks"	Plays with blocks
Perspective taking: Emotion cause-and-effect	"How can we make Sally happy?"	"We can surprise her with her favorite snack"
Dressing: Putting on shirt	Technician hands shirt to learner, says "Put your shirt on"	Puts on shirt
Planning	"Johnny is coming over to play soon, what should we do to get ready?"	"We could get out some paint and paper to paint on, replace the batteries in the video game controller, and pump up the tires on the bikes"

you are not clear on what response you should be looking for from the learner, ask the supervising BCBA before running the program.

Use common sense. Be flexible with what you accept as a correct response if the learner is demonstrating the skill, but in a slightly different way than you expect (e.g., a child is identifying a label whether she points to it or hands it to you).

5.1.7 Reinforcement
A skill acquisition plan may or may not specify what particular reinforcers to use for that plan. This is because reinforcers for most skill acquisition plans should be changed frequently, depending on the moment-to-moment preferences of the learner (see Section 4.1.1). However, some skills always result in a particular consequence, by definition. For example, manding (requesting), by definition, is reinforced by the consequence that the learner specifies. When teaching a child to ask for milk, after the child says "Milk," "Milk please," or "I want milk," you would always give the child milk, as opposed to some other reinforcer that is unrelated to milk. The skill acquisition plan should also specify the schedule of reinforcement that is to be implemented for a target skill (see more in Section 5.3.3).

5.1.8 Prompting and Prompt Fading
Skill acquisition plans should determine the prompts to be used and the prompt fading procedure. Prompts and prompt fading are discussed in greater detail below.

5.1.9 Teaching Targets or Exemplars
Virtually all of the skills you will teach learners with ASD have multiple different targets or exemplars you will need to teach. For example, when teaching functional pretend play, you might teach a learner to make a toy truck go "vroom," pretend to eat with toy food, pretend a doll is sleeping, make toy airplane fly, and so on. Sometimes these many different target component skills will be listed on the skill acquisition plan but often there are too many to list and so they may be contained on a separate document, sometimes called an "ideas sheet," "target list," or something similar. Appendix A is a sample.

5.2 SESSION PREPARATION

In most treatment programs, you will have some brief amount of time at the very beginning of the session when you have the opportunity to review all of the learner's skill acquisition plans, behavior intervention plans, and notes from recent sessions. In addition, use this time to gather all necessary teaching materials, datasheets, and get them all in position so that you are ready to teach the learner rapidly and effectively.

> Always remember that every moment is a teachable moment. Ensure that a learner is engaged in something functional while you prepare for session. Continue to engage the child as you prepare and be ready to intervene if challenging behaviors arise.

5.3 CONTINGENCIES OF REINFORCEMENT

Positive reinforcement is the basis of everything we do in ABA. Positive reinforcement is the basic concept that explains why people do what they do throughout their everyday lives. Positive reinforcement is the primary source of motivation for all of human behavior and for everything we try to teach in ABA programs for individuals with ASD. Before we get to the technical definition of positive reinforcement, it is useful to think about the following general concept: the consequence of behavior matters. The consequence of everything we do affects how we do it and whether we do it in the future. Some consequences are highly motivating. Some consequences have a very large effect on our behavior, even so large that we may only have to learn a lesson once. For example, you do not have to put your finger in an electrical outlet twice to learn that you should not put your finger in an outlet. Other consequences have a very small effect on a behavior or no effect at all. Reinforcement is a type of consequence that, by definition, has an effect on behavior in that it makes you do that behavior more in the future. Behaviors that result in highly desirable outcomes are likely to be repeated again in the future. If you drive a particular route to work and you experience very little traffic, you are likely to drive that route again in the future, compared to other routes with more traffic. Stated in more technical terms, *reinforcement* is a consequence that results in an increase or maintenance in the future probability of a behavior. Put another way, reinforcement is a consequence that strengthens behavior.

Reinforcement is not bribery. A bribe is where you give someone a reward *before* they do a behavior, usually a behavior that is morally questionable. Reinforcement is where you give a reward *after* a behavior and it is intentionally used to strengthen moral behaviors that benefit the learner.

Reinforcement works equally well on desired and undesired behaviors. For example, a child with autism might learn that when he asks for attention, he gets attention, and that may maintain that behavior in the future. However, depending on how adults interact with him, he might also learn that when he has a tantrum, he gets attention, and that may result in him having more tantrums in the future. Our job as behavior technicians is to ensure that adaptive behaviors are getting lots of reinforcement and maladaptive behaviors are not.

Another critically important thing to know about reinforcement is that it is completely idiosyncratic. In other words, what might be reinforcing to you will not necessarily be reinforcing to others. For example, you might love country music, whereas someone else hates it. The same may be true for broccoli, brussels sprouts, etc. Trains may be effective reinforcers for some learners with ASD, whereas stuffed animals may be effective for others. The only thing that makes something a reinforcer for someone is that it works to increase their behavior. Never assume something is going to be a reinforcer until you see it working.

5.3.1 Negative and Positive Reinforcement

So far we have learned that reinforcement is a type of consequence that increases the probability of a behavior in the future. Reinforcement can be further subclassified in terms of whether something is given or taken away from the person's environment. The term positive refers to something being given. The term negative refers to something being taken away. So, *positive reinforcement* is a consequence that is added to a person's environment that results in a future strengthening of that behavior. Common examples of positive reinforcement include getting access to social approval, preferred food, money, and so on.

Examples of Positive Reinforcement

- Child enters car calmly → Parent turns on child's preferred radio station
- Child raises hand quietly → Teacher calls on child to take turn
- Teenager calls to check in with parents on time → Is given extra time on curfew

- Child runs away when time to get in car → Parent negotiates and gives child choice of radio station in order to get in car
- Child calls out → Teacher calls on child to take turn

Negative reinforcement is the removal of a consequence that results in an increase in the behavior that resulted in that removal. For example, if music is too loud, then your behavior of turning the volume down gets negatively reinforced by having the excessively loud music removed from your environment. If a child with autism is asked to do work that he does not want to do and asks for a break and he gets a break, giving him a break (i.e., removing work) may negatively reinforce the child's behavior of asking for a break, which would be a good thing (i.e., asking for a break is better than engaging in destructive behavior).

Negative reinforcement... are you the nonpreferred stimulus being removed? Beware of creating a dynamic where the learner is motivated to earn escape from you and your teaching. Positive reinforcement should always outweigh negative reinforcement.

Examples of Negative Reinforcement

- Completes class assignment → Given break

- Puts head down when given class assignment → Sent outside/ given break

Negative reinforcement: Enough with the bad rap! "Negative" refers to something being removed, not the effect on behavior.

It is important to remember that both positive and negative reinforcement can increase either desired or undesired behavior. For example, if a child has a tantrum while in the grocery store and receives candy in order to be quiet, tantrums will likely happen again during future shopping trips, as it resulted in access to candy. Conversely, if the parent gives the child candy when he politely helps put the groceries away at home, polite behavior gets reinforced and will increase in the future. In this same example, negative reinforcement may be used as well. If the child had a tantrum because he did not like shopping, and his parent then took him outside the store, tantrums would likely be negatively reinforced and be more likely to occur in the future. However, if the shopping trip ended when the child waited calmly, the behavior of waiting would be reinforced. As such, negative reinforcement can increase either appropriate or inappropriate behaviors, depending on how we deliver it. To recap, positive reinforcement is when doing a behavior results in being given something preferred, while negative reinforcement is when doing a behavior results in taking away something nonpreferred. Both are reinforcement because they increase the strength of a given behavior.

Positive reinforcement	Preferred stimulus added	Behavior increases in the future
Negative reinforcement	Nonpreferred stimulus removed	Behavior increases in the future

5.3.2 Conditioned and Unconditioned Reinforcement

Another important distinction within reinforcement is the distinction between conditioned and unconditioned reinforcement. *Unconditioned reinforcement* is where the effectiveness of a reinforcer does not depend on a learning history. Instead, that consequence is a reinforcer simply due to genetics and natural selection in the evolution of the species. Examples of unconditioned positive reinforcers are food when a person is hungry (i.e., food deprived), water when a person is thirsty (i.e., water deprived), warmth when a person is cold, and sweet and salty flavors. Examples of unconditioned negative reinforcers are escape from extreme temperatures, escape from loud noises, and escape from physically painful stimuli. All of these are unconditioned reinforcers because people did not need to learn for them to become reinforcers, they are reinforcers for all humans (aside from very extreme cases).

Reinforcers that have acquired their effectiveness because of the learning history of the person are called *conditioned reinforcers*. They are reinforcers that are acquired during the lifetime of the person and they vary greatly from person to person. For example, although most people like sweet foods (unconditioned reinforcer), some people prefer one type of candy while others prefer another. Similarly, one person may prefer country music while another may prefer rap music. And one person may prefer broccoli, while another may prefer carrots, while a third person may hate all vegetables. There is nothing in the genetic makeup of these different people that determines which of those stimuli will be reinforcers. Instead, these different people have learned to prefer these different reinforcers because of their learning history.

The most common way in which stimuli become conditioned reinforcers is by being paired with existing reinforcers. The classic example that you may have heard of is "Pavlov's dog." Pavlov, a Russian researcher in the early 20th century, was the first scientist to document that, when a dog repeatedly contacts a neutral stimulus (bell) immediately before a strong stimulus (food), then the bell comes to have some of the functions of the strong stimulus. Specifically, after the bell had been paired with the food multiple times, when the dog only heard the bell, he would salivate, showing that pairing the bell with the food made the bell have some of the same effects on behavior as the food.

The principle of respondent conditioning was first demonstrated with dogs, but it turns out that this fundamental principle of learning works with almost every other animal on the planet, including human beings.

For example, a particular food or drink that you had at particularly reinforcing times in your childhood (e.g., lemonade on summer vacation) may still be a powerful reinforcer for you because of that history of pairing with pleasant events in your past. A major goal of working with learners with ASD is to establish stimuli for which the learner is not motivated at first (e.g., attention) to be reinforcers by repeatedly pairing them with stimuli that are already reinforcers (e.g., video games, food, etc.). For this reason, it is usually a good idea to praise the learner when you give her a reinforcer. By repeatedly praising when you give reinforcers, you are pairing praise with potent reinforcement and are therefore conditioning praise to be a reinforcer in the future.

Tokens. Token reinforcement is a common method for maintaining motivation with learners with ASD. *Tokens* are conditioned reinforcers that the learner earns for correct responses, which she can exchange later for more powerful reinforcers. For example, in an integrated preschool for children with and without ASD, a teacher might give students a point each time they follow an instruction the first time it is delivered. Once a student earns 10 points, she may then pick a "treasure" from the "treasure chest," a box that contains toys. When doing discrete trial training with a young learner with autism, it is common to create a "token board," which is a board or a piece of laminated paper that has space for a specified number of tokens to be earned. When the board is full of tokens, the learner can then trade it in to earn a larger reinforcer. This larger reinforcer is called the *backup reinforcer.*

Making the tokens themselves interesting or preferred may enhance the effectiveness of a token economy. For example, using stickers of a learner's favorite cartoon as tokens may work better than using completely neutral stimuli, such as poker chips.

Guidelines for Effective Use of Tokens

- Follow the rules for earning tokens in the skill acquisition plan accurately (e.g., every time the learner does one specific behavior, she earns a token)
- Make sure the learner sees that she earned a token (it is often a good idea to give it to her and have her place it in the jar, on the board, or wherever else tokens are stored until they are exchanged for a reinforcer)
- Give the learner the token *immediately* after the behavior that meets the criterion

- Follow the rules from the skill acquisition plan for when the learner is allowed to exchange her tokens (e.g., after ten tokens, she chooses a backup reinforcer)

Examples of Token Economies:

- Filling a sticker chart with stickers of the learner's favorite characters
- Completing pieces of a puzzle of a learner's favorite animal
- Adding marbles to jar
- Building rings of a stacking toy
- Receiving coins to make a purchase

5.3.3 Continuous and Intermittent Schedules of Reinforcement

The timing and frequency with which you give reinforcement is called the *schedule of reinforcement*. There are two basic schedules of reinforcement: continuous and intermittent. With *continuous reinforcement*, a particular behavior results in a particular reinforcer every time the behavior occurs. *Intermittent reinforcement* schedules are schedules in which a particular behavior produces a particular consequence, but not every time the behavior occurs. It is commonly believed that intermittent schedules of reinforcement lead to strong behavior maintenance. This point is important to consider when approaching desired as well as undesired behavior; we want to be sure we continue to reinforce desired behavior on a thinned schedule, but we want to be careful of intermittently reinforcing undesired behavior.

Continuous Reinforcement: "Every time I do this, I get what I am after!"

- Each bite of broccoli → Bite of chicken nugget

- Every time child throws food off of plate → Given alternate food

There are four types of intermittent schedules of reinforcement: fixed ratio, variable ratio, fixed interval, and variable interval. The schedule determines which occurrences of the target response will be followed by reinforcement. *Ratio schedules* of reinforcement specify how many occurrences of a target response are required before reinforcement is delivered. A *fixed ratio (FR)* schedule of reinforcement is when a reinforcer is delivered after a set amount of target responses. For example, after every five correct responses during DTT, the learner earns a 1-minute break (FR5). A *variable ratio (VR)* schedule of reinforcement is when a reinforcer is delivered after an average number of occurrences of the target response. For example, after an *average* of five correct responses in DTT, the learner earns a 1-minute break (VR5). Sometimes the learner may only need to complete three correct responses, sometimes four, sometimes six, and sometimes seven, but the overall average number required to earn a break is five.

Intermittent Reinforcement: "Sometimes this works to get me what I want, I'll give it a try!"

- Eats all his veggies → Given dessert every "few" nights
- Raises hand in class to give answer → Called on every "few" times
- Asks for desired item in calm voice → Given requested item some of the time

- Teenager repeatedly throws pencil while doing difficult homework → Eventually sent to room without having to finish work
- Student constantly calls out → Teacher finally calls on and allows answer to be given
- Child keeps grabbing toys from peers → Occasionally this results in access to toys

Schedules of reinforcement that specify the amount of time that must pass since the last reinforcer was given, before the behavior can be reinforced again are called *interval schedules*. A *fixed interval (FI)* schedule of reinforcement is when a behavior is reinforced after an established "fixed" amount of time since the last reinforcer was given. For example, a child may need to wait at least 5 minutes after her last break before she can ask for a break again (FI5). If she asks for a break earlier than that, there is no penalty, but she simply does not get the break. In other words, the first time she asks for a break after

5 minutes have elapsed since her last break, she gets a break again. A *variable interval (VI)* schedule of reinforcement is when the first occurrence of a target response is reinforced after an *average* amount of time. For example, the number of minutes that the learner would have to wait since her last break might change each time, from 3 to 7 minutes, but on average 5 minutes overall (VI5).

Example of Schedules of Reinforcement in Action

Dinnertime
- Fixed ratio
  - Continuous FR1 = every bite of broccoli results in bite of French fry
  - FR2 = every 2 bites of broccoli results in bite of French fry
- Variable ratio
  - VR3 = On average, every 3 bites of broccoli results in bite of French fry

Independent Play
- Fixed interval
  - FI 5 minute = After playing independently for at least 5 minutes, mommy will come play with Sally if Sally asks her
- Variable interval
  - VI 5 minute = After playing independently for between 3 and 7 minutes (5 minutes on average), mommy will come play with Sally if Sally asks her

---

5.3.4 Tips for Effective Delivery of Reinforcement
- *Immediate.* You should give the learner the reinforcer as quickly as possible after the behavior you are trying to reinforce occurs (e.g., within 1 second, if possible).
- *Enthusiastic.* Make sure to be upbeat and enthusiastic when you use praise as reinforcement.
- *Contingent.* Make sure the learner really needs to do the behavior to get the reinforcer. If the learner can get the reinforcer for free without doing the behavior you are trying to reinforce, then your reinforcement procedure will not work as well.
- *Large Enough.* Make sure the amount of the reinforcer you are giving is big enough for the reinforcer to be effective. For example, 30 seconds of a videogame might not be long enough for the game to be fun and it might not be an effective reinforcer, whereas a minute or 2 minutes might be enough.

- *Specific.* It is usually a good idea to name the behavior when you give reinforcement (e.g., "Check you out, you got your shoes!").
- *Use Expansions.* When reinforcing verbal behavior, it is often a good idea to model expansions of the verbal behavior you are reinforcing. For example, if you are giving the learner a reinforcer for labeling a red dog "red," you might say, "That's right it's a red *dog"* rather than just saying "That's right, it's red."
- *Maximize Motivating Operations.* For a reinforcer to work best, the learner should not have already received a lot of it recently (see Section 5.4).

5.4 MOTIVATING OPERATIONS

Antecedents can have a powerful effect on whether or not consequences are effective reinforcers. For example, if you already ate an entire chocolate cake for breakfast, then chocolate cake will likely not be a powerful reinforcer after dinner that night. Antecedents that affect the potency of reinforcers are called *motivating operations.* Motivating operations are divided into two types: (1) Establishing operations and (2) abolishing operations. *Establishing operations* increase the potency of a reinforcer and temporarily evoke behaviors that have been reinforced by that consequence in the past. For example, if an adult with autism has not eaten in a few hours, food becomes a stronger reinforcer and she is likely to ask for food or engage in other behaviors that have gotten her food in the past.

The most common type of establishing operation is *deprivation* and it simply means not having a reinforcer for some time. The term deprivation sounds negative or unethical but its technical meaning in ABA is not. It is merely a name for what happens to most of us every day. Every day when we wake up, we are food deprived because we have not eaten for a long time. Food is therefore a strong reinforcer first thing in the morning for most people. Then, if you eat breakfast, food loses some of its power as a reinforcer. Then, by noon or so, food becomes a stronger reinforcer because you have not eaten since breakfast (assuming you did not snack in the meantime), so you are food-deprived again. Deprivation is not a negative thing, it is simply a name for the normal day-to-day and hour-to-hour changes in potency that happen to reinforcers when we have not had them for a while.

Of course, some antecedents do the opposite of establishing operations. *Abolishing operations* are antecedents that decrease the potency of a reinforcer and temporarily suppress behaviors that have earned that reinforcer in the past. For example, if an adolescent with autism has just finished a large glass of water, water is no longer a powerful reinforcer at that moment and she is not likely to ask for water. Later on, if she has not had water again for a long time, then the lack of water will be an establishing operation (water deprivation), which makes water a powerful reinforcer again. *Satiation* is the term that refers to having had a reinforcer recently, and therefore the reinforcer becomes less powerful. So, if you want to make a reinforcer more powerful (e.g., for teaching), use deprivation, and if you want to make a reinforcer less powerful (e.g., to prevent challenging behaviors to get that reinforcer), use satiation. Chapter 6, Behavior Reduction, describes in more detail how to use satiation to decrease challenging behaviors with a procedure called noncontingent reinforcement.

> Consider the learner's recent history and how this may alter your teaching approach. Use antecedent modifications to set the learner up for success (e.g., snack if extremely hungry, demand fading if sleep-deprived, etc.).

5.5 DISCRETE TRIAL TRAINING

DTT is among the most well-researched and well-known treatment and education procedures for teaching skills to learners with ASD. *DTT* is a teaching method in which learning trials are presented in quick succession, with a clear beginning and clear end to each trial. There are three parts to a discrete trial: (1) the instruction delivered by the technician, (2) the learner's response, and (3) the consequence delivered by the technician. Skills commonly taught via DTT include matching, basic listener responding (e.g., identifying labels of objects or following simple instructions), motor and vocal imitation, language skills involving actions, features, functions, cause-and-effect, categories, and academic skills, including letters, numbers, shapes, and colors.

The rationale behind DTT is that learners with ASD often require a large number of learning opportunities to master skills and DTT was developed to ensure the highest number of learning opportunities possible.

The benefits of DTT are that it produces rapid learning, many learning opportunities can be presented quickly because learning is teacher-directed, it helps individuals with ASD to learn structured work expectations, and it is straightforward to train staff to implement. Potential drawbacks of discrete trial teaching include that it can teach rote responding if done poorly, that learned skills may not generalize to the less-structured natural environment, and that it does not build in reinforcement for learner spontaneity, per se.

General characteristics of most DTT skill acquisition programs:

- *The interaction between behavior technician and learner is broken down into three discrete units.* Trials consist of (1) the instruction delivered by the technician, (2) the learner's response, and (3) the consequence for the learner's response, which is delivered immediately by the behavior technician.
- *Teaching in DTT tends to be more structured.* There is a predictable back-and-forth between the behavior technician and the learner. This does *not* mean that teaching needs to be robotic or rote, merely that there is predictable structure.
- *The reinforcers used in DTT can be unrelated to the skills being taught.* Any reinforcers that are potent can be used in DTT, regardless of whether they are related in any meaningful way to the skill being taught.
- *Prompting is used to help learners respond correctly and prompts are then faded out.*
- *Trials are initiated by the behavior technician.* The behavior technician who is teaching the learner with autism specifies when each trial begins by gaining the learner's attention and presenting an instruction.
- *DTT tends to be fast-paced.* The behavior technician maximizes the number of trials she conducts and minimizes the amount of time the learner has to wait between trials.

Some people are unfamiliar with high quality DTT and refer to all DTT as "drill and kill," meaning that DTT hurts a person's motivation to learn because it is repetitive and boring. However, nowhere within discrete trial teaching protocols are behavior technicians instructed to be boring, use an artificial tone of voice, deliver repetitive and ineffective reinforcers, or use nonmeaningful teaching materials. Like everything else in ABA, DTT should be fun, upbeat, and motivating for the learner. For example, if teaching colors, you could present a trial for the learner to sort toys into piles based on color and then give the learner the toy they want from one of the piles as the reinforcer for that trial.

5.5.1 Implementing Discrete Trial Training

1. *Gain the learner's attention.*
2. *Deliver the instruction.* State the instruction in a clear and upbeat manner, not robotically. There is no need to use an artificial tone of voice.
3. *Pair a prompt with the instruction, if it is to be a prompted trial.* See prompting section below.
4. *Wait up to 3 seconds for the learner to respond.*
5. *If the learner responds correctly, reinforce immediately and enthusiastically.* Deliver whatever reinforcer you identified through a very recent brief multiple stimulus preference assessment (see Section 4.1.1).
6. *If the learner responds incorrectly or does not respond, implement a correction procedure.* The specific correction procedure will be specified by your BCBA (see Section 5.3.2).
7. *Record data quickly.*
8. *Gain the learner's attention again (if necessary) and present the next instruction.* The time from the consequence of one trial to the instruction on the next trial, called the *intertrial interval*, should be as short as possible (no longer than 3 seconds).

 DTT should be FUN! Keep the pace of teaching fast, while also:

- Being animated
- Sitting at places aside from a table (e.g., bean bag, floor, sofa, play structure)
- Embedding learning within play
- Using reinforcers that are related to the context and activity
- Varying praise

5.5.2 Error Correction Procedures

When the learner makes an incorrect response during DTT, you will generally implement a correction procedure. For example, you might repeat the instruction while also giving an immediate full prompt, to ensure the learner makes a correct response with the next learning opportunity. Different schools and agencies use different error correction procedures but the general rationale is to use prompting to prevent the learner from making repeated errors.

5.5.3 Mastery Criteria
The mastery criterion is the rule for how to decide when a particular skill or a particular phase of a skill acquisition program is mastered, based on the accuracy of the learner's performance. For example, after a child has demonstrated at least 90% correct in identifying the body parts, "hand," "tummy," and "head," in random rotation, with at least two different behavior technicians, and across at least two different days, we might say that those three targets have been mastered with that particular instruction. Different schools and service providers have slightly different mastery criteria but most are somewhere at or above 80% correct or greater across at least two different behavior technicians and two different days. Some BCBAs prefer 90% or higher, across 3 days. Make sure to check with your supervising BCBA.

5.6 NATURALISTIC TEACHING PROCEDURES

ABA teaching can also look natural in its delivery and can be embedded within play or everyday routines. A variety of naturalistic teaching procedures have been developed and shown to be effective with learners with ASD. Naturalistic teaching procedures are known by several names including: natural environment training, pivotal response training, milieu teaching, and incidental teaching. Each version of naturalistic teaching has its own unique characteristics and we do not have enough space for a thorough review of each. However, most naturalistic teaching procedures include the following common features: child-directed learning, use of reinforcers that are related to the teaching interaction, motivation embedded within the teaching context, interspersal of mastered skills, and less of a focus on maximizing the greatest possible number of learning opportunities (although this goal is not neglected).

5.6.1 Implementing Naturalistic Teaching
To implement naturalistic teaching, consult the skill acquisition plan. Each plan will specify unique details depending on the needs of each learner. However, the following steps generally apply to most naturalistic teaching methods:

1. *Prepare the environment.* Identify the skills to be taught and arrange the environment with the child's interests in mind, while still maintaining control over the particular opportunities that need to be contrived (e.g., preferred items out of reach, etc.). Arrange the environment accordingly before you are responsible for teaching the learner.

2. *Engage the learner in play/interaction in the arranged environment.* The goal is for the arranged environment to evoke an initiation by the learner (e.g., play next to the out-of-reach toy, give her a toy that needs batteries, give her paints without a paintbrush, etc.). Be sure to have the learner's attention and contrive a clear opportunity for the learner to respond.

3. *The learner initiates.* This is when the learning opportunity really begins. The learner might reach for the item, look at you expectantly, gesture, and so on. You are looking for some indication from the learner that she is motivated to interact with you (i.e., a strong motivating operation is present).

4. *If the learner's initiation is already sufficient for reinforcement, reinforce the response.* In other words, if the learner's first initiation is the target response, then reinforce it with a reinforcer that is related to the interaction. For example, if upon seeing that a paintbrush is missing from a paint set, a learner says to his behavior technician, "Paintbrush please," the behavior technician would give him a paintbrush.

5. *If the learner's initiation is not sufficient for reinforcement, prompt a response.* For example, if the learner's first initiation was to reach for a paintbrush but not say anything, the technician might use an echoic prompt by saying, "Paintbrush."

6. *If the learner responds to your prompt correctly, reinforce it and fade the prompt over time.* See section on prompting and prompt fading for techniques for this.

7. *Ensure that the environment is arranged for another learning opportunity.* This ensures that more than one learning opportunity can be conducted. For example, you could allow the learner to use the paintbrush for 30 seconds and then say, "My turn" and take a turn, thereby creating another opportunity for the learner to ask for it.

Naturalistic teaching can be used to teach a large variety of skills. For example, if you were teaching colors, and the child you were working with loved balloons, you might sit with her in front of a pile of uninflated balloons of different colors. When she reached for one of the balloons, that would be an opportunity to prompt her to ask for which balloon she wants by stating the color. The reinforcer for her correctly labeling a color would be you blowing up that balloon and giving it to her.

 Naturalistic teaching may look like play, but it should always include effective prompting and contingent reinforcement

Independent living skills can also be taught using naturalistic teaching procedures. For example, if going outside to play is a powerful reinforcer for a learner, then you could use going outside as an opportunity to teach him how to put on his shoes. To do this, you might tell the learner, "Alright, let's go outside and play!" while walking with him toward the door. At the last second before opening the door, you might say "Oops," and point toward his bare feet and the shoes sitting next to the door. You could then use a prompt to help him put his shoes on and then go with him outside to play, thereby reinforcing the behavior of putting on his shoes.

As stated earlier, many versions of naturalistic instruction exist and depending on which BCBA is supervising your work, there will be slight differences in how you implement the steps above. For example, in pivotal response training, it is common to reinforce an attempt at a correct response, even if it is not an improvement upon previous performance. Other versions of naturalistic teaching will specify the correct response you should reinforce. Make sure to consult with the skill acquisition plan and the supervising BCBA to ensure that you are implementing the program as designed.

Potential benefits of naturalistic teaching include better generalization, collateral improvements across untargeted skills, and possible preference by learners and their family members. Potential drawbacks to naturalistic teaching may be that it relies on a learner's motivation (which can be especially difficult for learners with ASD who demonstrate restricted interests), it requires planning and the ability to amend teaching on the spot by the behavior technician, and finally, treatment integrity as well as consistency across behavior technicians may be more difficult.

5.6.2 Balancing Discrete Trial Training and Naturalistic Teaching

Most top-quality ABA programs for learners with ASD today carefully assess what combination of DTT and naturalistic teaching are appropriate for each individual skill being taught to each learner. With most learners you work with, you will likely do a combination of DTT and naturalistic training for teaching skills. Broadly speaking, DTT is what ensures a large amount of practice and naturalistic teaching is what ensures that the learner can demonstrate the skill in their natural environment (i.e., generalization).

A great way to ensure that a learner gets enough structured practice and enough generalization is to frequently alternate back and forth between DTT and naturalistic teaching. For example, if you are teaching a young child with autism the names of body parts, you might first run a block of discrete trials, where you point to your head and deliver the instruction, "What's this?," where the expected learner response is "Head." When the learner makes a correct response, you would reinforce it with whatever reinforcer the learner is working for, e.g., praise, tokens, high fives, tickles on his head, etc. On subsequent trials in that block, you might do the same but for your arm and tummy as well. After completing a reasonable amount of work in discrete trial (e.g., maybe 5–15 correct responses, depending on the learner), you might then give the learner a break. During the break, you could then play with the learner on the floor and contrive ways for the learner to label those same body parts in order to get a natural consequence that is a powerful reinforcer. For example, if tickles are a strong reinforcer for that child, you might tickle her arm for a second and then stop and give an "expectant" look and shrug, as if to say you don't know what she wants. If the learner then says, "arm," you would tickle her arm. If she does not say arm, you would prompt her to say it, perhaps by modeling the word "arm." If she then says the target response or some approximation, you would then tickle her arm. You would then do the same for other body parts, all embedded within the fun activity of tickles.

Most top-quality ABA programs for children with autism alternate frequently from more-structured DTT to less-structured naturalistic teaching if a learner is observed to benefit from both types of teaching. The client learns that the day is made up of a back-and-forth "dance" between behavior technician and learner, frequently switching from more structure to less structure. In addition to ensuring lots of practice and lots of generalization training, this frequent shift in format helps prevent child and behavior technician from becoming bored and helps the child become more flexible with transitions, which is a challenge for many children with ASD.

 Learning opportunities matter. It is the job of the behavior technician to ensure quality and quantity.

5.7 SHAPING

Sometimes you will need to create new topographies or forms of behavior that you cannot yet reinforce because they are not occurring. *Shaping* is a procedure in which you reinforce successive approximations to a behavior, in order to create new forms of behavior. You start by reinforcing a form of behavior exhibited by the learner that is closest to the terminal behavior you are trying to establish. For example, when a learner with autism is learning his first few words, he may not be able to pronounce a whole word and you may need to start by reinforcing some small approximation of the word. For example, if an apple is an effective reinforcer and you are teaching the learner to say "apple" to request (mand) apples, you might start by giving the learner an apple when he says "a." After several successive sessions or days of reinforcing "a," you might then only reinforce "a-puh," and then later the full, correctly pronounced word, "apple." Your supervising BCBA will specify which particular approximations of a behavior to reinforce and the criterion for moving from reinforcing one approximation to another.

5.8 TASK ANALYSIS AND CHAINING

When teaching complex skills to individuals with autism, it is often useful to break the skills into smaller, more teachable steps. A *task analysis* (TA) involves breaking down a complex skill into small, teachable steps, which make up a *behavioral chain* of sequential responses to create a complex behavior. For example, to wash your hands, you likely do something like the following chain of behaviors: Turn on the water, wet hands, get soap, rub hands together, rinse hands, turn off water, dry hands with a towel. When teaching a complex behavior chain, the first step is to create a TA that specifies the sequence of shorter behaviors that make up the longer, complex behavior. The BCBA supervising a learner's program may start with an existing TA (e.g., from a previous learner or from a curriculum) or create a customized one for each task and/or learner.

Prompting and reinforcing each behavior in a TA is a teaching procedure called *chaining*. There are three variations to chaining: (1) forward chaining, (2) backward chaining, and (3) total task presentation. *Forward chaining* is where the initial step in the behavior chain sequence is taught first, while the behavior technician prompts or completes the remainder of the steps. To teach the first step, give the initial instruction and give the learner an opportunity to respond. For example, you would take the learner to a sink and say, "Wash your hands" and then wait for the learner to turn on the water (the first step in the chain). If she does so independently, you would then prompt her through the rest of the steps in washing her hands and then deliver positive reinforcement when she is done. If she did not do the first step independently, you would provide a prompt (e.g., physically guide her hands to turn on the faucet). After several days or sessions of doing this, the learner will start to complete the first step independently and you will then focus on teaching the second step, and so on, until she can wash her hands without help. Fig. 5.2 depicts forward chaining with use of a TA for teaching the skill of tooth brushing.

Instead of teaching the initial step first, some BCBAs prefer teaching the last step first so that independent responding with the natural completion of the task is immediately followed by reinforcement. *Backward chaining* is where all steps within the behavior chain are prompted by the behavior technician other than the final step, which is taught to the learner. For example, for hand washing, you would prompt the learner through all of the steps until the very last (drying hands) and you would then stop prompting and wait for the learner to independently dry her hands. If she does, you would deliver positive reinforcement. If she does not, you would prompt her to do so and then deliver reinforcement. After several sessions or days, the learner will start to dry her hands independently. You can then give her the opportunity to do the second-to-last step (turning off water) independently, and so on, for the rest of the chain.

Some BCBAs prefer teaching all steps in a chain at the same time. *Total task presentation* involves presenting the entire task to the learner and having her complete all of the steps until the chain is learned. For

Client: Joey Jet   Date: January 1ˢᵗ, 2016   Setting: Home

Technician: Annie Smith   Program: Self Help- Brushing Teeth

Instruction: "Brush your teeth?"   Response: Martha brushes her teeth.

Step	Target Behavior	Level of Independence
1	Get toothbrush	(0) 1 2 3 4
2	Wet toothbrush	(0) 1 2 3 4
3	Get toothpaste	0̶ (1) 2 3 4
4	Put toothpaste on toothbrush	0 1 (2) 3 4
5	Brush bottom teeth	0 1 (2) 3 4
6	Brush top teeth	0 1 (2) 3 4
7	Brush teeth on right side	0 1 (2) 3 4
8	Brush teeth on left side	0 1 (2) 3 4
9	Brush front teeth	0 1 (2) 3 4
10	Spit out toothpaste	0 (1) 2 3 4
11	Rinse mouth	0 (1) 2 3 4
12	Put toothbrush away	0 1 (2) 3 4

Summary: 2 / 12 x 100 = 17%

0= Independent
1= Gestural Prompt
2=Partial Physical Prompt
3=Full Physical Prompt
4=Verbal Prompt

Figure 5.2 Sample task analysis data sheet using forward chaining.

example, you would deliver the instruction, "Wash your hands" and watch what the learner does. You allow her to complete the chain of behaviors independently until she makes an error or does not respond, at which point you prompt to complete the current step correctly and then stop prompting and watch what she does next. In other words, you are using the least amount of prompting necessary to help the learner complete all the steps in the chain. Reinforcement is then delivered after completing the final step in the chain (drying hands).

Sample skills commonly taught using TA and chaining:

- Washing face
- Brushing teeth
- Dressing and undressing
- Making a sandwich
- Tying shoes
- Setting the table

5.9 DISCRIMINATION TRAINING

In ABA, the word discrimination means the ability of a learner to understand the difference between two or more things. For example, if we have taught someone to label red things as "red" and blue things as "blue," then we can say that we have taught the learner to discriminate between red and blue. Almost all language involves discriminations of some kind. For example, when you want milk, you ask for "milk," not water, and vice versa. You call your mother, "Mom" and your father, "Dad" and not the other way around. In typical development, you can watch these basic discriminations form very early, as children pick up the earliest forms of language. In the beginning, very young children often mix up their discriminations and those errors decrease over time as they learn the discriminations more firmly. The learning process is the same for children with ASD, except that it can be difficult and require more learning opportunities and more practice before the children master the skill. Some adolescents and adults with ASD never had those opportunities and may still lack some basic discriminations. Our job as behavior technicians is to engineer the learner's environment, whether they are young or old, to maximize their learning of fundamental language discriminations.

Everything that you learned in the sections on DTT, naturalistic teaching, and chaining above, involved teaching discriminations. For example, when teaching a learner their phone number in DTT, when you deliver the instruction, "What's your phone number?," you are teaching them to respond with their phone number, not their address or some other response. Or when teaching a learner to ask for a teddy bear when he wants a teddy bear in naturalistic instruction, the learner should say, "Bear" and not "Fire truck" or some other label. Finally, when using chaining to teach a learner to make a sandwich, the client learns to spread peanut butter on the bread, and not hot sauce or some other incorrect response. So, when you really think about it, virtually all learning involves learning discriminations because you are learning to do a particular behavior, not some other behavior, and/or you are learning to do something in the presence of one stimulus, and not another stimulus.

5.9.1 Stimulus Control

When a particular behavior has been reinforced only in the presence of a particular stimulus or instruction, that behavior begins to occur reliably in the presence of that stimulus or instruction, and we say that stimulus now has *stimulus control* over that behavior. For example, an adolescent with autism may learn that one particular staff person gives him attention when he uses foul language, and so the adolescent may now use foul language when that staff person is present. Or a child with ASD may learn that her grandmother lets her out of doing something she doesn't like to do when she has a tantrum. During an instructional session, we may therefore observe that the learner's grandmother comes over and upon seeing her, the learner immediately tantrums and the grandmother comes and hugs the learner and gives her a break from the task. In this example, the grandmother had acquired stimulus control over the learner's tantrums.

5.9.2 Discriminative Stimulus

Stimulus control applies equally to desired and undesired behavior. When we are effective as behavior technicians, our instructions begin to acquire stimulus control in that our clients learn that, in our presence, desired behavior gets reinforced, and so they learn to reliably engage in those behaviors when they see us. A stimulus that has come to have stimulus control over a behavior is called a *discriminative stimulus*, or "*Sd*" for short. For this reason, it is common to hear people refer to the instruction in a discrete trial as the "Sd," because the goal of DTT is to establish instructions as discriminative stimuli. In other words, the goal of DTT is to teach the learner that, when they hear a particular instruction, they should engage in a particular behavior, thereby establishing a discrimination. Of course, when you first begin teaching a new skill in DTT, the instruction is not a discriminative stimulus at all, because the learner has not yet learned the discrimination. But over the course of DTT, the instruction becomes an Sd as the learner acquires the discrimination. Below, we describe some procedures that have been developed to teach discriminations in DTT.

5.9.3 Simultaneous Discriminations

Some discrimination training procedures teach the learner to make discriminations between two or more stimuli that are present at the same time and these are called *simultaneous discriminations*. An easy way to think about simultaneous discriminations is that they are like multiple-choice questions on a test. An example of a basic simultaneous discrimination procedure is teaching matching skills. You might put a fork, knife, and spoon on a table, hand another spoon to the learner, and then deliver the instruction "Match" or "Put with same." The expected response would then be for the learner to put her spoon with the spoon on the table and not with the fork or the knife.

A more advanced discrimination would be a "receptive" discrimination (aka, listener behavior, or auditory-visual discrimination). For example, you might put a fork, a knife, and a spoon on the table and deliver the instruction "Where is the spoon?," "Give me the spoon," "Touch spoon," "Point to spoon," or simply, "Spoon," where the expected learner response would be choosing the spoon by pointing to it or giving it to you. Receptive (aka, listener, or auditory-visual) discriminations can be much more complicated, e.g., by asking about functions or features (e.g., "Which one do you scoop with?" or "Which one has tines?").

Steps in simultaneous discrimination training. Each service provider or school that you work in will have slightly different methods for teaching DTT simultaneous discriminations. If you simply conducted discrimination training as described above, it would probably work eventually but it would be difficult for the learner. Most service providers or schools have intermediate steps that make learning the discriminations easier. Since it is not possible for this book to describe all possible sequences of steps that all possible service providers and schools might implement, we describe a few of the most common ones here. Keep in mind the basic rationale behind all discrimination training is to make it as easy and fast as possible for the learner to learn the discriminations you are trying to teach. So generally speaking, all the different variations on discrimination training procedures start simple and gradually increase complexity until reaching the terminal discrimination.

Mass trials. Some agencies and schools begin DTT discrimination training with mass trialing. *Mass trialing* is a procedure where you present trials of the same simple discrimination repeatedly. For example, you might put a toy dog on the table (with no other toys present) and present the instruction, "Touch dog," where the expected learner response is to touch the dog. You would then repeat this same trial several times in a row, while reinforcing correct responses. It is extremely difficult for the learner to make an error in this situation because there isn't anything else present for the learner to touch and this is why many BCBAs feel this step may not often be useful or meaningful. Many service providers or schools do not use mass trialing and many only use it when learners have particular difficulty with early stages of discrimination training. Your supervising BCBA will tell you whether to implement mass trials for each individual learner and skill you are teaching.

Mass trial with a distractor. The next step in difficulty from mass trialing is to mass trial with one other stimulus present. For example, you might place a picture of a happy face and a picture of a sad face on the table and present trials where you only ask "Point to happy," while changing the position (left or right) of the two pictures frequently after trials, so that the learner is not merely learning to respond to the left or right position. The distractor stimulus (the one you are not asking for) can be either previously known or not previously known to the learner. Previously known stimuli will usually be more distracting (more difficult) than unknown ones. Again, your supervising BCBA will tell you whether to implement mass trialing with distractors for each individual learner and skill you teach.

Random rotation. To teach discriminations using *random rotation*, you put two or more stimuli out and randomly alternate between asking for the different stimuli. For example, you might put a larger and a smaller cup on the table and present the instruction "Which one is bigger?" or "Which one is smaller?" on randomly alternating trials. You would also change the position of the cups after each trial. This is the purest test of discriminative ability and therefore is the most difficult level of discrimination. Some BCBAs believe you should proceed straight to this step when teaching new discriminations and some believe you should do some amount of mass trialing or mass trialing with distractors first. The best strategy likely depends on the learner and the particular skill you are teaching. Your supervising BCBA will make this decision in each individual case.

Random rotation can be made more challenging by adding more stimuli for the learner to choose from on each trial. Presenting at least three stimuli is generally considered the standard for a stringent test of whether the learner has really acquired the discrimination, but four or five stimuli can be included to make the test even more stringent.

5.9.4 Successive Discriminations

Many discriminations do not involve choices between simultaneously available stimuli. *Successive discriminations* involve doing one behavior in the presence of one stimulus, and then doing another behavior in the presence of another stimulus at a later time. For example, you deliver the instruction, "Tell me something that flies," where the expected learner response might be "bird," "plane," or anything else that flies. On the next trial, you might deliver the instruction "Tell me something that swims," where the expected learner response might be something like "fish," "whale," or "I do."

To teach successive discriminations in DTT, you can mass trial many in a row of the same target before teaching another target or you can move immediately to random rotation, where you alternate trials of one target with trials of another target in random order. Or you can do something in between, where you might repeat one target until the learner makes an independent correct response, and then you might switch to the other target. Your supervising BCBA will specify what strategy she wants you to use with each learner and skill you are teaching.

5.10 PROMPTING

A prompt is something that you do to help a learner do something that they otherwise would not or could not do. In technical behavior terminology, a *prompt* is a supplementary stimulus that is used to occasion a response. By definition, a prompt is not the eventual stimulus that you want to control the behavior when you are done with teaching. Prompts are extra sources of help that need to be faded out in order for an individual to function independently. For example, when teaching greeting skills, you might initially need to prompt a learner to say, "Hi" to someone when the person walks through the door. Clearly, if that learner continued to need you to tell him to say "Hi" every time someone enters the room, the skill has not actually been learned. For him to successfully benefit from that teaching procedure, your prompt must be successfully faded. First we will describe each commonly used type of prompt, and later we will describe how to fade them.

5.10.1 Physical Prompt
A *physical prompt* is a prompt in which you provide some amount of physical assistance in order to help the learner do the expected behavior. Physical prompts can be further classified by the amount of physical assistance given. *Full physical* prompts are where you give the

learner full physical guidance. For example, when teaching a child to follow an instruction to put a doll in its cradle, you might deliver the instruction, immediately followed by a full physical prompt to help the learner respond correctly. A *partial physical* prompt is a physical prompt in which less than the full amount of physical assistance is provided. In the example just described, a partial physical prompt might be to assist the learner in picking up the doll and guiding his arm toward the cradle, and then letting go of the learner. *It is important to note that physical prompting is not the same thing as physical restraint.* Physical prompting does not involve forcing the learner in any way or restricting the learner's movement.

5.10.2 Model Prompt
A *model prompt* is a prompt in which you demonstrate the desired response. For example, when teaching a learner with autism to wave when greeted, you may show her how to do this skill by doing yourself. Modeling prompts can be vocal or physical demonstration of the desired behavior, and can be further subdivided into partial and full models. For example, instead of fully modeling a wave upon greeting the learner, you may lift your hand slightly as a cue for her to wave.

5.10.3 Verbal Prompt
Supplementary words, instructions, or questions to assist a learner in demonstrating a correct response are called *verbal prompts*. For example, when teaching an individual with autism to brush his teeth, you may provide verbal prompts for each step (e.g., "Remember to spit the water"). Verbal prompts can also be full or partial.

5.10.4 Gestural Prompt
A *gestural prompt* is a prompt where you indicate the correct response by gesturing in some way. For example, when asking a learner to pass a fork during a meal, you may point to the requested utensil among those on the table.

5.10.5 Proximity Prompt
A *proximity prompt* is a prompt where you make the stimulus that corresponds to the correct response closer to the learner than other stimuli. For example, if you were teaching attributes of objects (e.g., heavy vs light) and put a feather and a rock on the table, you might put the rock slightly closer to the learner when you deliver the instruction

"Which one is heavy?" and you might put the feather slightly closer when you deliver the instruction "Which one is light?"

5.10.6 Visual Prompts

Visual prompts are often used to help learners with transitions and schedules. For example, your supervising BCBA might create a visual schedule that depicts the sequence of events to take place during a therapy session, alternating between work and breaks, followed by lunch, followed by more alternating work and breaks, followed by a trip to the park, and so on. The various activities are generally depicted by photographs or icons, displayed in the sequence in which they are going to occur. To use a schedule such as this, you would show the learner the schedule and perhaps prompt him to point to each photograph or icon and name it—if he has the verbal ability to—during each transition during the session. These schedules can also be made into books, often called "picture activity schedules." The books have several pages, each of which has one picture that corresponds to one activity, thereby depicting a chain of behaviors. The last page of the book has a picture or icon that depicts a highly preferred reinforcer, which is the reinforcer for engaging in the whole chain of behaviors. To use a picture activity schedule, you prompt your learner to point to the pictures before engaging in each behavior in the chain and then give her reinforcement for completing all the activities in the chain. Essentially, picture activity schedules are like an adapted form of a to-do list and can be very effective in helping individuals with ASD manage their own behavior over longer periods of time and over complex chains of multiple different activities.

5.10.7 Extrastimulus Versus Intrastimulus Prompts

Extrastimulus prompts are any prompt where the source of the prompt is outside of the stimulus that you want the learner to respond to. This includes almost all prompts. For example, when pointing to a correct stimulus, your finger is physically outside of the stimulus you are pointing to. Or when modeling physically guiding a learner to clap her hands when she sees someone else clap their hands, your physical guidance prompt is coming from outside of her hands and the other person's hands.

Intrastimulus prompts are any prompts where the source of the prompt is within the stimulus that you want the learner to respond to.

Intrastimulus prompts involve modifying aspects of stimuli to increase the likelihood of the learner making a correct response. For example, when teaching a learner how to draw a circle, instead of modeling the response and drawing it yourself (which would be an extrastimulus prompt), you could have a circle to trace prewritten on the paper. Another common situation to use intrastimulus prompts is when you over-emphasize certain parts of words in your instruction. For example, when teaching a learner to understand plural words, you might put a single car on one side of the table and then a pile of cars on the other and deliver the instruction "Point to cars" on some trials and "Point to car" on other trials, thereby requiring the learner to discriminate between "car" and "cars." To use an intrastimulus prompt, you might over-emphasize the "sss" sound at the end of "cars" by delivering the instruction, "Point to carSSSS." Another situation in which you could use an intrastimulus prompt is to increase the size of the stimulus that you want the learner to respond to, compared to the other stimuli. If you were teaching categories, you might put a picture of a dog, a truck, and a couch on the table and ask the learner to identify the animal, vehicle, or furniture on alternating trials. To use an intrastimulus prompt, you could have larger versions of each picture that you use only when you are asking for that particular stimulus (e.g., put out the larger picture of the truck when you are asking for vehicles).

5.11 PROMPT FADING

Prompts are extra help and it is critical that they are faded out quickly and effectively so that the learner with autism does not become dependent upon them in order to respond. For example, when teaching a learner to sit still on the rug during circle time, the behavior technician may have introduced a small carpet with the learner's name as a prompt to sit still on his designated spot. Once the learner is doing so successfully, it is time to systematically fade that prompt. First, the technician may fade the size of the carpet smaller and smaller as the learner is successful. Then the carpet may be removed altogether so that the general learning environment now acquires discriminative control of the learner's sitting behavior.

There are multiple ways in which prompts can be faded out. Fading prompts is one type of *stimulus fading*, a procedure where some aspect of a stimulus is slowly and systematically faded. With all prompt fading procedures, you move from providing more prompts early on in learning to providing fewer later on, until the learner responds correctly and independently without your help. Generally speaking, prompts can either be faded out on a least to most (LTM) or most to least (MTL) basis.

5.11.1 Least to Most Prompt Fading

LTM prompt fading includes procedures where fewer prompts are provided at the beginning of a teaching interaction and gradually more intrusive prompts are faded in when the learner needs help. For example, you may present the instruction "where is your tummy," when teaching a learner to identify their own body parts. You may provide no prompts when initially delivering instruction, and then if the learner does not respond correctly to the instruction within a few seconds, you may then represent the instruction and immediately give a model prompt by touching your own abdomen. If the learner still does not respond correctly after a few seconds, you may then represent the instruction again and immediately following it with a physical prompt where you physically guide her hand to touch her own tummy.

5.11.2 Most to Least Prompt Fading

MTL prompt fading works in the reverse direction. With MTL prompt fading, you begin the teaching interaction by providing a prompt that you are sure is likely to help the learner make a correct response, and then fade those prompts out as the learner continues to respond correctly. The previous example could also be taught using MTL prompting. For example, you would present the first instruction, "Touch tummy," and immediately physically prompt the learner to touch her abdomen. On the following trial, you might say the instruction and then provide only a model prompt. If the learner responds correctly, on the next trial, you would present the instruction without a prompt. MTL prompt fading can also be done across successive teaching sessions. For example, you might teach five trials of a particular skill using physical prompting in the morning, and then five trials of that same skill using partial physical or model prompting in the afternoon, and then five trials with no prompting the following morning.

Time delay. There are numerous options of how to fade prompts. One option is to insert a delay that occurs after the instruction, but before the prompt. For example, when running mand (requesting preferred items/activities) training on the first learning opportunity of a particular day, you might present full prompts immediately. If a child was reaching for his favorite bear, you might withhold the bear and present an immediate full vocal model prompt and then wait for a correct vocalization from the learner, at which point you give him the bear. If the child responds correctly and gets the bear, you might then let him play with the bear for approximately 30 seconds to 1 minute. You might then remove the bear until the child initiates toward the bear in someway. Instead of an immediate full vocal model as you did on the first learning opportunity, you might delay your vocal model by 1 second while raising your eyebrows as if to give the learner an expectant look. If the child says, "Bear" after your delayed prompt you would then give him the bear for another 30 seconds to play with. You might then remove the bear while increasing your delay to providing a full vocal model by one more second after each successful learning opportunity. After several such learning opportunities, you will be waiting up to 5 seconds or more before providing the model. You are thereby giving the learner a greater and greater opportunity to respond independently.

It is often useful to fade prompts by using a combination of fading the level and fading the delay. For example, on trial one, you might provide a full physical prompt, on trial two you might provide a partial physical, on trial three you might provide a 1 second delay to the partial physical, on trial four you might provide a 2 second delay to the partial physical, and on trial five you might provide no prompt at all.

It is important to keep in mind that there is no right or wrong way to fade prompts. The way that you know you are using an appropriate procedure for fading prompts for a particular skill and a particular learner, is that you are able to fade prompting successfully and the learner is able to continue to respond correctly without your assistance. In other words, a particular choice of a particular procedure for fading prompts is right if it works. You should also keep in mind that the BCBA who is overseeing the learner's program is responsible for tailoring prompt fading procedures to use with that learner. Some organizations have standardized, structured procedures for prompt fading that they attempt to follow across all learners and other organizations leave it up to the behavior technician to use their knowledge of prompt fading to choose the most appropriate prompt to use in the moment.

Regardless, make sure that the method you are using follows what the BCBA overseeing that particular case prescribes for that program.

Prompt dependence is a term used to describe a situation in which a learner continues to need a prompt in order to respond correctly even after repeated unsuccessful attempts at fading those prompts. Look out for prompt dependence, as it is quite a bit more common than you would like. If you notice that a learner seems to be falling into a routine of simply doing "whatever she normally does" and continues to require assistance from you and other caregivers, even after she has "mastered" a skill, consider whether prompt dependence may be developing and alert your supervising BCBA.

5.12 STIMULUS CONTROL TRANSFER PROCEDURES

There are many situations where one stimulus reliably evokes a behavior, but you want another stimulus to do so because the second stimulus is the one to which the learner must be able to respond independently in everyday life. The examples of prompt fading described above are all such cases. A prompt is one stimulus that reliably controls a response, but you want a different stimulus to control that same response. For example, an adolescent with ASD who regularly fails to wash his hands after using the bathroom. The father notices this and so the father regularly reminds him when he comes out of the bathroom to go back and wash his hands. So, the stimulus that controls hand washing is the father's prompt, whereas the stimulus we would like to control hand washing is the sight of the sink immediately after using the toilet. We would say that we would like to *transfer stimulus control* from the unwanted prompt to the desired stimulus in the natural environment. There are many ways that this can be done, but generally speaking, they involve fading out the father's prompt and/or prompting the learner to orient to the desired stimulus. For example, the father or an instructor may point to the sink immediately after the learner finishes with the toilet but before he exits the bathroom.

It is often necessary to transfer stimulus control from one person to another. For example, the team of behavior technicians may have successfully decreased a child's escape-motivated tantrums (see chapter: Behavior Reduction), but the child may still engage in the same type of tantrums with parents who have not yet implemented the new behavior intervention plan. To transfer stimulus control of low rates of tantrums from the behavior technicians to the parent, you might gradually fade control from the technician (you) to the parent. For example, you might have the mother be physically present while you implement the intervention plan 1 day, then have the mother implement instructions while you implement consequences the next day, then have the mother implement all parts of the plan with you present the following day, and finally have the mother implement all aspects of the plan with no behavior technicians present, until tantrums remain low with the mother. The entire process may then need to be repeated with the father and any other relevant caregivers. In practice, the supervising BCBA will plan and supervise this process, but you may well have the opportunity to participate.

5.13 GENERALIZATION PROCEDURES

Generalization is the spreading of the effects of training from the training setting or behavior to other settings or behaviors. ABA services cannot possibly take place during all times and settings for the vast majority of learners with ASD, and so it is absolutely critical that ABA treatment produces generalized gains, so that the learner is able to apply the skills she learned in therapy to all relevant aspects of her life. Generalization is not an afterthought or side effect; it should be thought of as the central goal of treatment.

Generalization can be divided into two types: (1) stimulus generalization and (2) response generalization. *Stimulus generalization* is where a particular behavior is trained in the presence of one stimulus and then it occurs in the presence of other stimuli that are physically similar. For example, if you teach a child to label (aka tact) pictures of apples as "apple," and the child is then also able to label actual apples as "apple." Another example of stimulus generalization may be if you taught a learner to identify siblings' and parents' emotions accurately and then he correctly identifies peers' and teachers' emotions. *Response generalization* is where one particular behavior is trained in the presence of a stimulus and then a different behavior occurs in the presence of that stimulus. For example, if you have taught a learner to build a house with a set of blocks, and then he spontaneously builds a different house or a boat with the same set of blocks.

5.13.1 Multiple Exemplar Training

Perhaps the most reliable way to get generalization when teaching learners with autism is multiple exemplar training (MET). *MET* is when you teach more than one example of the skill or concept you are trying to teach. For example, when teaching a learner the label, "dog," you may show her a picture of a dog, point out dogs while on a walk, read a book with dogs, and watch cartoons with dog characters. In the presence of each of these examples of dogs, you might point to the dog and present the instruction, "What is it?", where the expected learner response would be "dog."

Training lots of exemplars is critical, but in order for MET to be effective, you need to keep training more exemplars *until you see generalization to untrained exemplars.* The supervising BCBA should specify what exemplars to use and how many to use for each individual skill acquisition plan. Some teaching approaches and curricula based on Relational Frame Theory, e.g., *PEAK Relational Training System* (Dixon, 2015), make establishing generalized skills a central focus. Such approaches use MET from the start of teaching and testing for generalization to untrained exemplars is part and parcel of everything you teach all day. Generally speaking, the more you use, the better generalization you will get but the more difficult it might be for the learner to learn at first. With many learners with autism, it can be more effective to start teaching a new skill with just a few exemplars and increase the number as the learner progresses through the program. Regardless, you aren't done teaching additional exemplars until the learner demonstrates accurate responding with new exemplars you have never trained.

5.13.2 Training Across People and Settings

Many learners with ASD will not generalize across people and settings unless a particular skill is trained across multiple people and settings. This is why it is crucial for a learner's treatment team to include more than one behavior technician. This is also why it is crucial for parents and other caregivers to be included in the treatment team and to practice newly learned skills with their son or daughter on a frequent basis. Treatment and education must also take place in multiple settings, in order to ensure generalization across settings. For example, if you are implementing treatment in the home, then do not always do therapy in one particular room and make sure to practice newly learned skills in other appropriate community settings (e.g., park, restaurant, etc.). If you are implementing treatment in a clinic or school setting, make sure to move to different parts of the classroom or to different classrooms and to practice skills during recess and lunchtime and on the playground, in the cafeteria and any other available settings.

5.14 MAXIMIZING LEARNING OPPORTUNITIES

Now that you know the major procedures to make learning happen with learners with ASD, there is one more thing you need to know while you do it: Good ABA programs maximize learning opportunities. One of the most basic ideas behind ABA is that learning happens when the learner contacts an antecedent, makes a response, and then receives a consequence. To ensure that the most learning possible is occurring, present many quality opportunities to respond followed by powerful consequences. All other things being equal, if the learner contacts learning opportunities twice as fast, you should be able to make twice as much learning happen while you work with him. A good indication that you are making the most of a session is that you are tired and maybe even sweaty at the end of the session. Of course learners deserve breaks from instruction, but do not let time between learning go on for too long. If 3 minutes of free play would function as a reinforcer, then letting free play go for 10 minutes means that you have just thrown 7 minutes of potential learning in the trash. Make every second count!

5.15 MAINTENANCE PROCEDURES

Maintenance is when a skill acquisition or behavior reduction maintains across time, after that particular skill or challenging behavior is no longer being directly targeted. For example, when a learner continues to independently get ready for school each day after this is no longer a target within his skill acquisition program. Maintenance is equally critical to generalization. If a learner does not maintain the gains that he makes while working with us, then we are wasting his and your time implementing treatment, and condemning the individual to a lifetime of dependence on others. Luckily, several procedures are effective for encouraging maintenance and they are described below.

5.15.1 Intermittent Reinforcement

As described earlier in this section, intermittent reinforcement is when only some (i.e., not all) occurrences of a behavior are reinforced. Most of our everyday ongoing behavior is on some kind of intermittent schedule of reinforcement, so we need to teach the learners with ASD with whom we work to adjust to and rely upon intermittent reinforcement. To use intermittent reinforcement for encouraging maintenance, first check the maintenance section of the skill acquisition plan or check any existing separate maintenance plan. Generally speaking, reinforcement should be gradually thinned from continuous reinforcement during skill acquisition to reinforcing every other correct response, to reinforcing every two to three correct responses on a variable and unpredictable schedule.

5.15.2 Transitioning to Natural Reinforcers

The ultimate goal of thinning reinforcement is to gradually change reinforcement schedules so that the frequency, magnitude, and predictability of reinforcement naturally occurring in everyday life maintains skills. For example, social attention given from peers during play maintains a child's social initiations or a teacher's typical level of attention maintains a student's behavior of raising his hand during lessons.

Example of Thinning Reinforcement to Natural Schedule

Eating a new vegetable:

- Reinforcer following each bite (FR1)
- Reinforcer following average of 3 bites (VR3)
- Reinforcer following average of 5 bites (VR5)
- Reinforcer following average of 7 bites (VR7)
- Large reinforcer following entire portion consumed
- Medium reinforcer following entire portion consumed
- Small reinforcer (dessert) following entire portion consumed
- Small reinforcer (dessert) following entire portion consumed a few times per week

5.15.3 Maintenance Checks

Probing previously mastered skills on an intermittent basis is an important way of ensuring that skills are maintaining. Check a learner's maintenance plan for what to probe and how often and ask your supervising BCBA if the details are not clear. Do not prompt during maintenance checks, but do reinforce correct responding intermittently in order to help maintain good performance.

5.16 CAREGIVER AND STAFF TRAINING

Adequate caregiver and staff training is crucial for a learner's overall success. Both caregivers and staff can be trained via behavioral skills training (see more regarding staff training in Chapter 7). Entry level behavior technicians will not play a large role in training others, but may participate by collecting data, role playing, etc. As behavior technicians gain experience, they will likely take on more responsibility in modeling for and training caregivers and staff, while under the supervision of a BCBA.

CHAPTER 6

Behavior Reduction

Teaching skills is by far the most important part of applied behavior analysis (ABA) treatment and education for individuals with autism spectrum disorder (ASD). However, reducing challenging behavior is also critical because it often prevents an individual from learning new skills. Therefore, although the primary focus of education and treatment for individuals with ASD should always be establishing new skills, it is very often necessary to focus heavily on reducing challenging behavior early on so that treatment can become focused on skill acquisition.

6.1 ESSENTIAL COMPONENTS OF BEHAVIOR REDUCTION PLANS

A *behavior reduction plan*, also known as a *behavior intervention plan (BIP)*, is a document that describes the procedures you use to help the learner decrease their challenging behavior and choose more adaptive replacement behavior. Behavior reduction plans must be written clearly and must be accessible to all behavior technicians on the team. Fig. 6.1 is a sample behavior reduction plan. If you have not carefully reviewed a learner's behavior reduction plan, ask your supervising BCBA for time to read the plan before you work with that learner. A comprehensive behavior reduction plan must have, at minimum, the components described below.

6.1.1 Operational Definitions of Target Behavior

The plan must include objective, clear, and complete operational definitions of target behaviors and replacement behaviors (see Section 4.1).

6.1.2 Antecedent Modifications

A behavior reduction plan must describe the procedures that you implement *before* the target behavior occurs, in order to prevent the behavior. The most important antecedent modification strategies are outlined later in this chapter.

Training Manual for Behavior Technicians Working with Individuals with Autism.
DOI: http://dx.doi.org/10.1016/B978-0-12-809408-2.00006-4

BEHAVIOR INTERVENTION PLAN
Problem Behavior + Operational Definition
Aggression: Any instance of grabbing a person with one or both hands, scratching, pinching, pulling hair, hitting, and/or kicking, including all attempts.
Function
Escape/avoidance: Typically occurs in the home setting during tabletop tasks
Antecedent Modifications
Priming prior to transitions and changes in expectations Effective Instructions: clear explanation of expectations Task interspersal Choices NCR: Break (1 min) from tasks every 10 minutes Functional Communication Training (FCT) Visual Schedule
Replacement Behaviors
Compliance, Waiting, and Mands for Cessation
Consequence Manipulations
Escape Extinction + Differential Reinforcement of Alternative Behavior (DRA):
Block and redirect all attempts. Continue with activity in place prior to occurrence of noncompliance. Provide reinforcement of break contingent on compliance with tasks and appropriate requests for escape.
Measurement
Rate per hour

Figure 6.1 Sample behavior reduction plan.

6.1.3 Replacement Behaviors

A quality behavior reduction plan is incomplete if it does not identify particular replacement behaviors and how to increase them. Especially when a learner displays a lot of severe behavior, it is easy to focus only on the behaviors you are trying to reduce. However, it is equally or more important to remember the behaviors you are trying to increase because these are the behaviors that will allow the learner to continue to get what she wants, without having to resort to challenging behavior. Generally speaking, communication that allows the learner to access the same reinforcers that she was previously using the challenging behavior to get is the best. Replacement behaviors are discussed in greater detail later in this chapter.

6.1.4 Consequence Modifications

Behavior reduction plans must specify how you are to react to the target challenging behavior and to all other behaviors that may occur. When it is possible to implement, extinction is almost always the best consequence for a behavior you are trying to reduce (see Section 6.4).

6.1.5 Persons Responsible

Behavior reduction plans must clearly indicate who on the treatment team is responsible for implementing which aspects of the plan. Often, all team members are responsible for implementing the plan. If this is the case, then the plan might not explicitly state this, as it is assumed to be this way for all learners being served in that organization. In any case, the supervising BCBA should make it clear to you whether or not you are expected to implement the behavior reduction plan.

6.1.6 Emergency Measures

BIPs should specify what measures to take in case of a behavioral emergency. A *behavioral emergency* is an episode of behavior that represents a clear danger to the learner or others. *Emergency procedures* are procedures that you use only for the purpose of preserving safety in the moment and are not part of the therapeutic core of the treatment plan itself. For example, if the BIP includes attention extinction for attention-maintained aggression, but the learner's aggression sometimes reaches levels of intensity that will result in physical harm, additional procedures must be specified to prevent harm. For example, physically blocking the behavior or the use of padded protective equipment. The intervention plan should include clear instructions on any reporting that is necessary when emergency procedures have been used. We discuss emergency measures further at the end of this chapter.

6.1.7 Common Functions of Behavior

The *function of behavior* refers to the reason why the behavior is occurring and continues to occur, i.e., the source of reinforcement for the behavior. A very large amount of research has been conducted on the sources of reinforcement that typically maintain challenging behavior. It is important to know that every behavior is different and that the shape or topography of the behavior does not tell you why the learner is engaging in it (i.e., form does not indicate function). For example, if you want to open the door, you could turn the doorknob, which would result in opening the door, or you could ask someone else to open the door, or you could kick the door down. The three behaviors have completely different forms but they all produce the same result; i.e., opening the door.

Research has shown that more than 90% of challenging behavior displayed by people with developmental disabilities have one or more of four specific functions (Hanley, Iwata, & McCord, 2003). The four most common functions of challenging behavior are: (1) access to *attention*, (2) access to preferred *tangible* items or activities, (3) *escape* from demands, or (4) *automatic reinforcement*. Let's go over each of the four functions in greater detail.

6.1.8 Attention

Behaviors that have an *attention* function are behaviors that continue to occur because they help an individual get attention from others, a form of positive reinforcement. There are many reasons why someone would engage in challenging behavior to get attention. One reason is that the individual may not have other ways of communicating that he wants attention. For example, consider a child who does not have enough language to ask his father, "Play with me please." When the child wants attention because he has not had it for a while (he is deprived of attention), he may learn that when he misbehaves, he gets a large reaction. Unfortunately, the most common reaction to someone misbehaving is to reprimand them. As such, individuals with autism may receive some form of attention when they engage in misbehavior.

Common forms of attention include comforting or consoling, reprimanding or nagging, conversations about feelings and motivations, and so on.

It is important to note that we are not saying that people with developmental disabilities do not deserve attention. Quite the contrary. Individuals with developmental disabilities deserve frequent access to high-quality attention just like all other human beings. However, when attention is delivered as a consequence of misbehavior, it can accidentally reinforce that behavior and make the problem worse. Parents and staff often unintentionally give inadequate attention to individuals with ASD when they are *not* in crisis. Parents are often busy with other tasks such as bills, cleaning, cooking, and so on. Professional staff are often engaged in other tasks such as managing the behavior of other individuals, teaching other individuals, and so on. Individuals with ASD may learn that, if they do not misbehave, they receive little attention, whereas if they do misbehave, they get more attention. It then becomes the job of ABA treatment providers to teach the learner better ways to get attention. We will talk more about how to do this soon.

6.1.9 Tangible

The *tangible* function refers to behaviors that continue to occur because they help the learner get preferred items or activities, another form of positive reinforcement. Similar to attention, individuals with ASD may learn that they are more likely to get preferred foods, toys, or activities if they misbehave. A parent walking down the candy aisle in the grocery store is the classic example. Understandably, parents do not want their children to have a tantrum in the store, so they often accidentally reinforce tantrums by letting the child have the candy instead of waiting out the tantrum.

6.1.10 Escape

The escape function is exactly what it sounds like. Challenging behaviors that serve an escape function are behaviors that allow an individual to escape from things he does not want. *Escape* is a form of negative reinforcement, where a learner's challenging behavior causes other people to allow them to either avoid or escape something they do not want. The thing that the individual is trying to escape from can be completely different from learner to learner. Some things that individuals with ASD may want to escape or avoid are difficult academic work, self-care tasks, loud or intense noises or tactile stimuli, and many others. Keep in mind that the function of a behavior is unique to each individual so it is possible that learners you work with will use problem behavior to escape or avoid something that most people find positively reinforcing. So when considering function, always think about what is actually working from the learner's point of view.

The escape function can be divided into two different types: (1) escaping something the learner finds undesirable, and (2) avoidance of something undesirable that has not yet happened. Let's use the example of task demands to illustrate. Consider a mother who is trying to get her son with ASD to eat his dinner. If the child is already seated at the table with the food in front of him and his mother asked him to take a bite of broccoli and he screams and his mother then stops asking him to take a bite of broccoli and waits for him to calm down, then that screaming allows him to escape from the demand to eat broccoli that was already present. However, suppose the meal had not yet started and the learner's mother says, "In five minutes, we are having broccoli for dinner," and then Johnny screams and his mother postpones dinner for an additional 10 minutes in order to help him calm down. In this example the demand to eat broccoli was not present when screaming occurred, so there was no demand to escape from. Instead, screaming postponed the demand of eating broccoli for 10 minutes.

6.1.11 Automatic Reinforcement

All of the functions we have discussed so far consist of reinforcers that another person delivers to the learner as a consequence for the behavior. Automatic reinforcement is different. By definition, *automatic reinforcement* is reinforcement that is *not* delivered by someone else. It is reinforcement that occurs as a physical consequence of doing the behavior. For example, if a bug bite is itching and scratching the bite produces a pleasurable feeling, the pleasurable feeling is automatic reinforcement for the behavior of scratching. No other person is needed in order to deliver the pleasure that results from the scratch. Eating good food, reading a good novel, watching a good movie, and listening to preferred music are other common examples of behaviors that are automatically reinforced. However, remember that the function of a behavior is defined by what the actual source of reinforcement is, not by the form of the behavior. So, even though reading novels is often maintained by automatic reinforcement (we just do it because it feels good to do it), there are other circumstances in which that exact same form of behavior is maintained by different consequences. For example, in school one is required to read novels in order to pass a class.

According to the diagnostic criteria for ASD, individuals with autism have repetitive interests and/or engage in repetitive behaviors. Repetitive behaviors can range from very simple behaviors such as body rocking, to very complex behaviors such as having conversations about the same preferred topic over and over. Each individual with ASD is different and each repetitive behavior serves its own unique function, so you should not necessarily assume that repetitive behaviors are automatically reinforced. However, the vast majority of research on repetitive behaviors in individuals with autism has shown that it is usually automatically reinforced (Wilke et al., 2012). Common automatically reinforced behaviors include behaviors that produce visual stimulation such as gazing at ceiling fans, turning light switches on and off repeatedly, flapping hands in front of the eyes, and gazing out of the corner of the eyes. Common automatically reinforced behaviors that produce auditory stimulation include repeating the same nonfunctional noises, repeating the same verbal statements, and repeating lengthy sections of verbalizations from television programs and movies (often referred to as "scripting"). It is also very common to see highly restricted food preferences. For example, only eating foods with one particular texture, color, or food group.

6.2 ANTECEDENT MODIFICATIONS

Antecedent modifications change some aspect of the learner's environment to prevent challenging behavior. Antecedent modifications are important because they can help you avoid challenging behavior, rather than reacting to it. Antecedent modifications are proactive, not reactive.

6.2.1 Noncontingent Reinforcement

Noncontingent reinforcement (NCR) is a procedure where reinforcement is given to the learner for free, i.e., not contingent on any behavior. Instead, reinforcement is delivered according to the passage of time. Typically, the reinforcement that you deliver should match the function of the challenging behavior. For example, if an adolescent learner throws items in order to gain escape from tasks, you could give a 3-minute break every 15 minutes, independent of the learner's behavior. Or if a child with autism has learned to whine to get his mother's attention, NCR may be used to give him his mother's attention for 5 minutes every 30 minutes. In order to implement NCR, you will need some way of measuring time in order to follow the time-based schedule. You can use a stopwatch, timer, a smartphone, or even a wall clock may work if the intervals are long enough (e.g., 5 minutes or more in between reinforcement). To be the most effective, NCR should be implemented with extinction. That is, when the target challenging behavior occurs, you should not give the functional reinforcer as a consequence of that behavior. For example, if the child's mother is giving the child attention every 30 minutes for free, she should *not* also give him attention as an immediate consequence of his whining. Whining should produce no attention at all.

NCR is very effective at decreasing challenging behavior because it decreases motivation for the learner to use challenging behavior to get reinforcement. By giving lots of reinforcement for free, you are decreasing the value of that reinforcement (i.e., an abolishing operation). But keep in mind that, if you use NCR to decrease the value of a reinforcer, a learner may be less likely to engage in good behaviors to get that reinforcer as well.

Examples of Function-Based NCR:
- Attention
  - Teacher-delivered attention every 5 minutes, regardless of behavior
- Tangible
  - Continuous access to iPad while in grocery store
- Escape
  - Five minute play break outside every 30 minutes
- Automatic
  - "Squeezes" at end of each song during circle time

6.2.2 Demand Fading
Demand fading is a procedure where you initially decrease the amount of work that you ask the learner to do. For example, during dinner,

you may start by presenting a very small amount of vegetables and slowly increase the portion across successive days, as the learner is successful. This procedure is used to decrease behaviors that are maintained by escape from demands. By decreasing the amount of demands you present, you are making work overall less undesirable and therefore decreasing the motivation to escape (i.e., another kind of abolishing operation). To implement demand fading, check the BIP for instructions on how to determine the correct amount of work to ask the learner to do. Usually, you will need to check notes or datasheets from the previous session, so you can see what number of demands or amount of work was last done successfully. Once you have this information, you can use the criterion from the BIP to figure out whether to increase the amount of work or keep it the same (e.g., after two sessions in a row with tantrums at or below one per hour, increase the number of demands by one).

6.2.3 Task Modification

Changing some aspect of how you ask the learner to work is referred to as *task modification*. Task modification is another procedure used to decrease challenging behaviors that are maintained by escape from demands. By changing some aspect of the task in a way that makes the task more preferred by the learner, you decrease the learner's motivation to escape from it (i.e., another abolishing operation). There are many different ways to do this, including changing the task materials (e.g., identifying actual objects rather than pictures of objects), incorporating learner preference (e.g., allowing the learner to use a pencil with his favorite cartoon character on it, etc.), and many others.

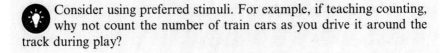 Consider using preferred stimuli. For example, if teaching counting, why not count the number of train cars as you drive it around the track during play?

6.2.4 High-Probability, Low-Probability Sequence

Using a *high-probability, low-probability (high-p, low-p) sequence*, also commonly referred to as a *behavioral momentum* procedure, involves asking the learner to do several tasks that she is likely to comply with (high-p tasks) before asking her to do one task that she is not likely to comply with (low-p tasks).

Examples of High-P, Low-P Sequences:

- Mealtime: Pasta, pasta, vegetable
- Homework: Several easy math problems followed by one difficult problem
- Following instructions: A few simple one-step instructions, followed by a more complex, two-step instruction

6.2.5 Choice

Frequently incorporating choice when working with a learner with ASD is likely to help decrease her motivation to engage in challenging behavior. To implement choice, simply let the learner choose aspects of the session that are possible for her to choose. There are many different ways choice can be built in. If two tasks need to be done, let the learner choose which is first or let the learner choose some aspect of how it is done. For example, when it is time to sit down, allow the learner to select the chair. For a writing task, let the learner choose between a pen and pencil. Even the simplest task can often have choice built into it. For example, instead of just telling a learner, "Turn on the faucet," you can ask, "Do you want to turn on the faucet with your right or left hand?"

Examples for Embedding Choice:

- Task: Transitioning inside from outside play
  - Possible choices: 1 or 2 more minutes of play, run or hop to the door
- Task: Completing puzzles
  - Possible choices: Which puzzle to complete, which piece to start with, where to complete the puzzle
- Task: Mealtime
  - Possible choices: Which bite to eat first, where to eat, where each food goes on plate, which utensil to use

6.3 DIFFERENTIAL REINFORCEMENT PROCEDURES

When you choose to reinforce some behaviors and not others, this is called *differential reinforcement*. Below, we describe three main versions of differential reinforcement, plus some of their subtypes, for decreasing challenging behavior.

6.3.1 Differential Reinforcement of Alternative Behavior

Differential reinforcement of alternative behavior (DRA) is a procedure where you reinforce one behavior and place another behavior on extinction (see Section 6.4). Generally speaking, the behavior you place on extinction is the target challenging behavior and the behavior you choose to reinforce is a particular alternative behavior that you reinforce with the same reinforcer used to maintain the challenging behavior. For example, if a learner with autism throws objects and the function is to escape from task demands, then you could implement DRA by no longer letting him escape from work when he throws objects (escape extinction) and instead give him a break from work when he completes some work (negative reinforcement).

Examples of DRA by Function:

- Attention
  - Talk to learner when she talks politely, do not talk to learner when she has a tantrum
- Tangible
  - Give the child a turn with a toy when she shares with others, do not give the child the toy when she hits peer to get it
- Escape
  - Give the learner a 2 minute break when she completes work require-ment, do not give her a break when she rips worksheet
- Automatic
  - Reinforce singing along with cartoon instead of out-of-context vocalizations

Functional communication training (FCT). Generally speaking, the best type of alternative behavior to reinforce when implementing DRA, is communication. *FCT* is a specific type of DRA, where you teach the learner to ask for what he wants, rather than using challenging behavior to get it. For example, for escape-maintained tantrums, you could teach the learner to make the manual sign for "break" and then give him a break from work when he makes the sign, and no longer give him a break from work when he has a tantrum.

Examples of FCT:

- Attention
  - Give learner attention when she points to desired item and do not give attention when she falls on the ground and cries
- Tangible
  - Give individual a magazine when he signs for it and do not give magazine when he tries to take it from a peer
- Escape
  - Give learner a 1 minute break when he asks for a break and do not give learner a break when he screams

Differential reinforcement of incompatible behavior (DRI). Another subtype of DRA is called *differential reinforcement of incompatible behavior*, a DRA procedure where the alternative behavior is physically incompatible with the challenging behavior.

Examples of DRI by Function:

- Attention
  - Reinforce polite requests for attention and do not attend to whining
- Tangible
  - Give learner more blocks when he plays nicely instead of grabbing toys
- Escape
  - Give learner a break when she completes work instead of when she destroys materials

6.3.2 Differential Reinforcement of Low-Rate Behavior

Some challenging behaviors are only a problem because they occur at too high a rate. For example, the skill of raising one's hand in class can become maladaptive if done too frequently. If you implemented DRA, it might eliminate hand-raising completely, which would be a negative effect on the child's behavior. A better choice might be *differential reinforcement of low-rate behavior* (DRL), a procedure where a target behavior is only reinforced if it occurs at or below a particular rate. For example, the teacher could call on the student only if it has been at least 5 minutes since the last time he raised his hand (e.g., reinforce the behavior only when it occurs at rates at or below once every 5 minutes and do not reinforce the behavior when it occurs more frequently).

Examples of DRL by Function:

- Attention
  - Reinforce five or fewer instances of calling out during class lesson with attention
- Tangible
  - Reinforce three or fewer instances of touching peers while waiting in line for lunch with access to being first in line
- Escape
  - Reinforce fewer instances of putting head down on desk during assignment by giving a break from work
- Automatic
  - Reinforce fewer instances of counting toy cars during recess with access to this routine after recess

6.3.3 Differential Reinforcement of Other Behavior

Differential reinforcement of other behavior (DRO) is a procedure where you only give reinforcement when the target challenging behavior does *not* occur for a specific amount of time. For example, a learner with autism may receive reinforcement following a specified amount of time without engaging in vocal stereotypy. To implement DRO, check the BIP to find out how long the behavior must be absent in order for the learner to earn reinforcement. This period of time is called the DRO interval. Usually, when you implement a DRO, you start with a very short interval based on the time between responses typically observed for the target response, as short as 5 or 10 seconds sometimes. If that works to decrease the rate of the challenging behavior, the BIP should specify how you will gradually increase the DRO interval (e.g., after two sessions in a row of less than five behaviors per hour, increase the DRO interval by 1 minute).

Examples of DRO by Function:

- Attention
  - Absence of whining for parent is reinforced with parent attention
- Tangible
  - Absence of grabbing others' toys is reinforced with access to preferred toy
- Escape

- Absence of protest is reinforced with a break
- Automatic
  - Absence of vocal stereotypy during storytime is reinforced with access to do so after storytime

6.4 EXTINCTION

Extinction is the basic principle that, states that behavior that is maintained by reinforcement will decrease when that reinforcement is discontinued. This basic principle of learning is a scientific fact that has been proven by hundreds of research studies and is also consistent with a common sense understanding of how rewards work. If reward motivates a behavior and then reward is no longer available, it makes sense that the behavior will decrease in strength over time.

Now let's consider what extinction looks like when you implement it to decrease challenging behaviors of learners with autism. Keep in mind that extinction means no longer reinforcing a particular behavior with the particular reinforcer used to maintain that behavior. There is no one correct way to do extinction across all behaviors because it completely depends on the function of the behavior. The proper way to implement extinction is dependent on what reinforcement previously maintained the behavior. Below, we describe how to do extinction for the most common functions.

6.4.1 Attention Extinction

Extinction procedures that are used to decrease behavior maintained by attention can be referred to as *attention extinction*. Consider the behavior of a child hitting his sibling. If the parents' reaction of reprimanding the child is the consequence that has been reinforcing the behavior until now, then extinction would consist of the parent no longer reprimanding the child for hitting. This does not mean the parents cannot intervene to keep the sibling safe, but in order for extinction to be effective, the parent would need to provide the least amount of reaction necessary to keep the sibling safe. For example, the parent could remove the sibling or the child from the situation or increase the distance between the two and pay lots of attention to the sibling while turning his or her back to the child who was hitting. However, if the same behavior was not maintained by the parents reaction but rather by the sibling's reaction, then attention extinction would consist of the sibling no longer providing the desired reaction but rather providing the least amount of reaction needed to keep him or herself safe, without providing the usual reaction of hitting back, arguing, name-calling, and so on.

Extinction is often confused with ignoring. If the maintaining reinforcer for a behavior is a reaction of some sort, then having no reaction whatsoever would indeed be extinction. But the particular type of reaction that is usually given to the behavior may be what the learner with ASD is looking for, so it may work to stop giving that kind of reaction and instead give the minimum amount of reaction necessary to keep everyone safe, without the usual argument, reprimand, and so on. And of course keep in mind that if the function of the behavior is not attention then ignoring the individual when they do the behavior is not extinction at all. Let's now turn to cases such as these.

6.4.2 Tangible Extinction

Tangible extinction is somewhat similar to attention extinction because they are both forms of extinction for behavior that is maintained by positive reinforcement; however, the source of positive reinforcement is different. *Tangible extinction* involves no longer providing access to preferred items or activities as a consequence of the behavior. For example, if a boy with ASD has a tantrum when his sibling plays with his toy, extinction would involve withholding his access to the toy during tantrum behavior. If a child is in the grocery store with his parents and the function of his crying is to get candy, then to do extinction, the parent would need to refrain from giving the child candy.

Tangible extinction is in many ways the easiest type of extinction to do because you can usually identify what the learner wants and simply not give it to her when she engages in the behavior. However, it can be difficult to implement when in public or when the learner escalates to behaviors that are dangerous. Even though it may be embarrassing and/or frustrating for behavior technicians or parents to allow the learner to escalate the challenging behavior and not give in, it is worth it because in the long run, the behavior will improve. If you choose to give in to the behavior, it is only more likely to happen again in the future and likely to become worse over time.

6.4.3 Escape Extinction

Escape extinction consists of no longer allowing an individual to escape or avoid something non-preferred (e.g., task demands) when they engage in challenging behavior. Put more technically, *escape extinction* is the discontinuation of negative reinforcement for a behavior. There are many ways in which you can implement escape extinction. The important thing to remember is that whatever demands were in place or were going to be placed when the behavior happened, must still be in place after the behavior. For example, if a mother asks her child with ASD to clean his room and the child screams, to implement escape extinction, the mother would need to continue to require him to clean his room until he does it, regardless of screaming. Similarly, if a child had a tantrum to avoid brushing his teeth, escape extinction would involve still having him brush his teeth while having the tantrum.

In some cases, physical guidance or physical prompts are used to prevent a learner from escaping a task. Escape extinction does not require *increasing* the amount of physical prompting used as a reaction to misbehavior, but rather simply doing the same thing the behavior technician was already doing when the behavior occurred. For example, if the behavior technician was already implementing a prompt hierarchy that included physical prompting, when the learner does not respond to an instructional task, the behavior technician would still implement those same physical prompts. It is important to note that the use of physical prompting and physical guidance has varying degrees of legality and restriction in different settings, for different behaviors, and in different states. In some states, physical guidance is outlawed except in behavioral emergencies (see Section 6.5.1). It is important to note that, if you are not permitted to implement physical guidance to ensure compliance with instructional requests, escape extinction may require some other form of disallowing escape. For example, if you ask a student to complete a worksheet and the student screams, "No!" and you cannot physically guide her complete the worksheet, then you may need to continue to present verbal instructions or just disallow access to any other activity until the worksheet is complete. In this case, the learner is able to escape the task in the short-term by simply refusing. However, if she is not allowed to engage in any other activity until the original task demand is complete, then overall, you are still disallowing escape.

6.4.4 Extinction of Automatically Reinforced Behavior

Extinction for automatically reinforced behaviors is much more difficult than extinction for behaviors that are maintained by attention, access to preferred items or activities, or escape. The reason for this is that behavior technicians do not control the source of reinforcement, so it is not possible for the technician to merely withhold reinforcement. In most cases, if the individual is free to engage in the behavior, then they are free to receive the reinforcement the behavior automatically produces. Therefore, extinction for automatically reinforced behavior involves identifying a way to allow the behavior to occur, but to prevent the behavior from producing the stimulation that normally reinforces it, often referred to as *sensory extinction*. Consider an example of an automatically reinforced behavior of hitting a table, where the source of automatic reinforcement is the noise the behavior produces. This behavior could potentially be put on sensory extinction by putting padding on the table to dampen the noise. In extreme cases of automatically reinforced self-injurious behavior, protective equipment sometimes effectively reduces the behavior through sensory extinction. For example, if an individual hits himself in the head and the maintaining reinforcer for that behavior is the sensory input that it produces on the learner's head, then requiring her to wear a padded helmet may reduce that sensory input because the padding absorbs much of the force of the hitting behavior, thereby reducing the feeling that the behavior produces on the person's head.

Two points about sensory extinction are critical. First, sensory extinction is *not* sensory deprivation. It is immoral and illegal to deprive a human being of sensory input. While sensory extinction attempts to eliminate the sensory feedback caused by one specific destructive behavior, it never involves eliminating that sensory input completely. For example, a blindfold could never be used to place hand flapping on sensory extinction because the blindfold would deprive all visual stimulation, and therefore would be a form of abuse, not sensory extinction. A second important point is that sensory extinction is not restraint. One common form of sensory extinction is called *response blocking*, which means using your own hand, arm, or a pad to block a learner from doing a behavior. For example, if a learner with ASD tries to slap herself in the face, then calmly and carefully blocking that behavior by placing your hand in between the learner's hand and her face would be a form of response blocking. This may serve as sensory extinction because it may stop the attempted slapping from producing the desired stimulation on the learner's cheek. However, when you do response blocking, you *do not* manually restrain or hold the individual's body, you merely block a behavior from occurring and then immediately remove your body or the pad you are using to block the behavior.

6.4.5 Extinction Bursts

When you first implement extinction for a particular behavior, it is likely that you will see an extinction burst. An *extinction burst* is a temporary increase in the rate or intensity of the behavior. As long as you continue to implement function-based extinction accurately, the undesired behaviors will decrease.

6.5 CRISIS/EMERGENCY PROCEDURES

Any time you work with learners who engage in behaviors that could pose a danger to themselves or others, it is important to have a plan for what to do when the behavior represents a significant safety threat. Behaviors that pose a threat to safety are *behavioral emergencies* and they must be planned for. A variety of different measures may need to be taken in behavioral emergencies. For example, manual restraint, protective equipment, or moving the learner to a different environment, are examples of emergency procedures. Do not be afraid to ask for help from any other staff or caregivers who are present, *before* the situation escalates out of your control.

Another important point to remember is that, when you are working with a client who is displaying aggression toward you, it is completely human to have negative emotional reactions. In the moment, you may become angry, scared, or take the client's behavior personally. However, regardless of how you feel on the inside, you must choose to respond professionally and without emotion on the outside. It is not personal, it is a job, and your job is to manage the situation safely and professionally. No matter how upset you are, there is never an excuse for aggression toward a client. If you assault your client, you will be terminated from your job immediately and you will be prosecuted for abuse. Behavior technicians assaulting clients is extremely rare but it has happened, just as it has happened with teachers, police, and others whose job it is to manage aggressive behavior. Do not let it happen to you.

As a behavior technician, it is not your job to plan for emergencies, i.e., the job of the BCBA. However, you should be certain that you know what to do if a behavioral emergency arises and ask your BCBA if you are not sure. It is also critical to note that it is your professional and ethical responsibility to treat all clients with the utmost respect and dignity at all times, even in behavioral emergencies. It is also your responsibility to be aware of local, state, and federal laws and agency and school policies regarding restraint, seclusion, and other emergency measures.

6.5.1 Emergency Behavior Management Training

Many commercially available trainings exist that train you in how to safely deescalate and manage behavioral emergencies. Your BCBA should arrange for you to receive one of these trainings. If you have not received this sort of training, ask for it. If you have not had intensive, specific, high-quality training in how to physically respond in a behavioral emergency, you will not be able to manage the situation safely. Get trained and keep your training up-to-date.

CHAPTER 7

Documentation and Professional Conduct

7.1 DOCUMENTATION

Documenting and reporting is a central part of behavior technician work. As we discussed in Chapter 2, Autism Spectrum Disorder, applied behavior analysis (ABA) is unique in how accountable we are for what we do and whether it works. In this chapter, we describe other forms of documentation, besides data.

7.1.1 Professional Language

It is critical to remain professional in all documentation and reporting. Occasionally, behavior technicians make the mistake of writing down personal anecdotes in professional documentation, such as talking about how the learner may be in a bad mood that day, how she is excited for the weekend, or the like. It is important to avoid such mistakes because it can be offensive to the learners and family members of the learners that you work with and it is unprofessional. Fig. 7.1 contains statements made in an unprofessional manner. Try to reword them professionally, without losing the intended meaning. Focus on nonevaluatively describing behaviors. Discuss your attempts at rewording with your trainer. When funding agencies (e.g., insurance companies) review documentation, they expect to only see a professional and complete record of what took place and if they see any other unprofessional communications, that can have a negative impact on the ability of the team to continue to have treatment funded by that agency.

7.1.2 Ecological Variables

During your session, you will need to record any ecological variables that might be important for caregivers or staff to know. For example, if the learner did not get enough sleep the night before, missed a meal, or skipped her medication, it might affect her behavior and so others need to know about it. Your supervising BCBA should provide you

Training Manual for Behavior Technicians Working with Individuals with Autism.
DOI: http://dx.doi.org/10.1016/B978-0-12-809408-2.00007-6

Unprofessional Language	Reword More Professionally
"I have no idea how to run that one." (when asked to model a specific program)	
"He gives me a really hard time."	
"I can't get anything out of her."	
"She was out of control today!"	
"I haven't run that program forever."	
"She doesn't pay any attention in music. It's a big waste of time."	
"That room is chaos." (school ABA room)	
"I do it totally different than Sally."	
"We don't have time to get anything done at school."	
"I had no idea what I was supposed to do."	
"It's no wonder he's still screaming a lot. His parents let him do whatever he wants outside of therapy."	

Figure 7.1 Samples of unprofessionally-worded language. Try rewording the statements more professionally and get feedback from your trainer on how you did. Reprinted with permission from Autism Bridges, Inc.

with instructions on where to record such information, such as in team notes, session notes, or the like.

7.1.3 Objective Session Descriptions

Many funding agencies require that each behavior technician record brief objective session notes after each session or shift. Each agency will likely have slightly different requirements but generally speaking, these notes provide a brief summary of what goals and behaviors were targeted and what was successful and what was not. Make sure to only include objective descriptions of what you actually observed, not guesses or inferences.

7.1.4 Team Communication

A good majority of your time will likely be spent working one-to-one with learners. However, the importance of remembering that you are part of a team and that the efficiency of that team directly influences a learner's progress cannot be overemphasized. Any time that more than one behavior technician works with a given learner, it is absolutely critical for the entire team to communicate effectively with one another. At the end of your session or shift, you will need to complete brief notes that provide essential information for the next behavior technician. For example, you might record which particular reinforcers you used, which skill acquisition programs you worked on, or if critical session materials are damaged or missing. Team communication notes sometimes overlap with objective session descriptions, described above, but usually team meeting notes are used for the internal communication of the team, whereas objective session descriptions may be used for documentation for funding agencies (e.g., insurance companies). In any case, make sure to ask the supervising BCBA exactly what elements are required for each type of documentation.

7.2 LEGAL, REGULATORY, AND WORKPLACE REPORTING

Each unique setting, city, county, state, and client population comes with its own unique set of laws and regulatory requirements. Each funding source has different requirements for reporting. Always check with your supervising BCBA to ensure that you are aware of the data collection and reporting requirements and that you follow them faithfully.

7.2.1 Mandated Reporting

Laws on mandated reporting vary a bit from state to state and vary considerably outside of the United States. However, in the United States, mandated reporting laws require that you report to the police or to child protective services (or adult protective services) if you have a reasonable suspicion that a child or vulnerable person (e.g., adult with disability, elderly person, etc.) is being abused or neglected. If you suspect that a child or vulnerable person is being abused or neglected, you must report it to the authorities immediately. Do not try to investigate the matter yourself and do not talk to the people who you suspect are perpetrating the abuse. If you are not sure if you should report something, make an anonymous call to the authorities and describe the situation and they can help you decide whether to file an official report. Failing to report suspected abuse is very serious. Not only could you allow a person to continue to be harmed, you can be arrested and face serious legal consequences. It is critical to familiarize yourself with mandated reporting requirements that apply to you.

7.2.2 Incident Reports

An *incident report* is a formal document that you use to report an unusual incident or accident that occurred during your session. The most common type of incident is learner or staff member injury. For example, if a child with autism bites a behavior technician on the forearm and the bite breaks the skin, the behavior technician would fill out an incident report to document the injury. Or if an adolescent with autism falls down and gets a bruise on his knee, the behavior technician would fill out an incident report to document the injury.

Each service provision agency will have its own forms for reporting incidents, but incident report forms generally require you to fill out at least the following information: (1) name of learner, (2) date, (3) your name, (4) setting in which the incident occurred, (5) who else was involved, (6) what was done to prevent the incident, (7) what was done as a reaction to the incident in the moment, (8) who was notified of the incident, and (9) what will be done in the future to prevent future incidents of this sort. It is important to only record what you objectively observed and to be honest and complete, so the responsible BCBA can take measures that will help prevent staff and learner injuries in the future. You have a moral and ethical obligation to report incidents honestly. You will also likely be terminated from employment if you report an incident dishonestly. Incident reports typically must be filed rapidly, usually within 24 hours.

7.2.3 Data Storage and Transportation

Proper data storage is important at all times. If practicing in the United States, you must adhere to federal HIPAA regulations when storing and transporting any sort of protected health information (e.g., a learner's full name, birthday, or address). When using electronic data collection, data storage will almost always occur automatically via a confidential database. When collecting data with pen and paper, there will be specific procedures for where datasheets are to be stored. Your supervising BCBA will specify these procedures, so check with her to ensure you are aware of the correct procedures. In most autism treatment and education programs, a learner will have her own logbook, clipboard, or folder that contains her blank and completed datasheets. Data should generally be kept in that specific location until the specified time that it is to be removed and taken to a location where it will be locked and stored longer-term. When datasheets are taken from their daily locations to storage, they should be taken quickly and directly to the storage location. Datasheets should not remain in unsecured intermediate locations, such as your car, any longer than is required to move them to the secured storage location. The secured storage location must be locked and must be located behind a locked door. For example, datasheets should be kept in a locked filing cabinet that is located in a room with a locked door.

7.3 PROFESSIONAL CONDUCT

Conducting yourself professionally and ethically is of the utmost importance. Appendix B contains an outline of the ethical codes from the *Professional and Ethical Compliance Code for Behavior Analysts* that specifically apply to RBTs (Behavior Analyst Certification Board, 2014b). We highly recommend you review these guidelines carefully and discuss them with your trainer. In your ethics training, your trainer should discuss common examples of problematic situations that correspond to each of the ethical guidelines and discuss common solutions and safeguards. After you become an RBT, we highly recommend you return to the ethical guidelines on a regular basis, as a set of guiding principles in your daily practice.

7.3.1 Role of the Behavior Technician

The role of the behavior technician is to implement behavioral education and treatment plans designed by BCBAs. It is not the responsibility of the behavior technician to design or create your own intervention plans. If you are not clear on what to do with a particular learner, you should not make your own decisions, you should ask your supervising BCBA. This is not because your opinions and experience are not relevant. In fact, you may often know the learner much better than the supervising BCBA since you spend much more time with him or her. Instead, the reason is because the BCBA has specialized training that you do not yet have on how to create, customize, and adjust skill acquisition and behavior reduction plans. When you have ideas that you think would be relevant, you should share your ideas with your supervising BCBA. The BCBA will inform you of the appropriate format for sharing your ideas. For example, comprehensive skill acquisition programs for children with autism are often supervised during regularly occurring team meetings.

Even though you may feel enthusiastic and it may be tempting, do not try out your ideas without checking with the supervising BCBA first. If you do, you can create inconsistency in the learner's program and her challenging behavior and/or skill acquisition may be affected and the BCBA will not be able to determine why the change occurred, because you did not inform her that you were doing something differently.

Although it will not be your job to make supervisory decisions, there will be times when situations arise for which your supervising BCBA has not told you exactly what to do. In situations where someone's safety is at risk, if you do not know what to do, you must choose the action that is most likely to keep everyone safe. For example, if a learner's behavior intervention plan does not specify what to do if she runs away, and she runs toward a busy street, you obviously must physically stop her from running into the street into the dangers of passing cars. You would need to use the least amount of physical force necessary to prevent her from entering the street (e.g., placing your body between her and the street, etc.). In short, when you are not sure what to do, use common sense and prioritize safety above all else, and immediately inform the supervising BCBA.

7.3.2 Receiving Performance Feedback

All people are capable of learning. This applies for the learners with whom we work and to staff at all levels, from entry-level behavior technicians, to BCaBAs, to BCBAs, and to BCBA-Ds, of all ages and experience levels. Therefore, a huge part of your job as a behavior technician is to constantly be on the lookout for ways in which you can improve in helping your learners to achieve their greatest potential.

Luckily, decades of research have repeatedly demonstrated that a few basic procedures are effective in making you the very best you can be at your job.

Initial training: behavioral skills training (BST). As we have already mentioned, this manual is just one part of a top-quality initial training program for behavior technicians. In addition to reading this book, you must go through BST to learn how to actually implement all the procedures described in this book. *BST* is made up of a sequence of three steps: (1) verbal explanation, (2) modeling, and (3) rehearsal or role-play with feedback. The verbal explanation component of staff training comes from reading this book and through lecture and discussion with the BCBA or BCaBA who is conducting your 40-hour behavior technician training. Modeling is where the BCBA or BCaBA demonstrates how to implement a procedure, usually with you or another trainee pretending to be a learner with autism. Rehearsal or role-play with feedback consists of the trainer then pretending to be a learner with autism and you act out the procedure you are being trained on, as if you were working with a learner with autism. As you role-play the procedures, the BCBA or BCaBA gives you immediate and specific feedback on your performance. You then continue role-play with feedback until you demonstrate excellent performance and no longer require feedback. The final stage to demonstrate mastery is to implement the same procedures with a real learner with autism, while a trainer watches and provides any help that is needed. After you have demonstrated all competencies accurately while working with real learners with autism, an evaluator will use the *Registered Behavior Technician (RBT) Competency Assessment* (Behavior Analyst Certification Board, 2016) to conduct a field evaluation to evaluate your performance and document that you have demonstrated all needed behavior technician task list competencies. Appendix C is a sample field evaluation developed for a trainer to use to evaluate behavior technician performance in the school setting (Quigley, Blevins, & Trott, 2016).

Ongoing performance management: goal setting and feedback. After you pass your field evaluation, you will be assigned to work with learners with autism and you will be entrusted to implement the procedures contained in the learners' programs with high accuracy. However, merely knowing how to do something is not enough.

Decades of research have shown that all humans require ongoing good-quality supervision to maintain excellent performance. The most important part of good-quality supervision is that it provides meaningful and effective antecedents and consequences for your work behavior. In particular, your supervising BCBA will provide you with ongoing immediate, specific, positive feedback when she observes you implementing behavior technician procedures well. For example, upon observing you implementing reinforcement immediately and enthusiastically with a learner, your supervising BCBA should in turn provide you with specific praise for your behavior. In addition, your supervising BCBA will provide you with immediate, specific, corrective feedback when she observes you implementing procedures incorrectly or with poor quality. Corrective feedback usually includes verbal explanation and modeling, when needed. For example, if upon observing you provide too few learning opportunities and deliver reinforcement for undesired behavior, the supervising BCBA should clearly explain how more learning could have been presented and exactly when and how undesired behavior was reinforced. Further, specific feedback on what you should do to improve your behavior technician procedures should also be delivered.

Let's face it: no one wants to receive corrective feedback. But if you want to be great at your job, there is no getting around the need for ongoing supervision and feedback. No one is perfect. The most competent behavior technician is the one who acknowledges that she is not perfect and seeks out feedback to become better. A wise mother of a child with autism once said, "Check your ego at the door. It's not about you and it's not about me. It's about my child. What we do affects his future and we have got to get this right. It's not personal." So when your supervising BCBA gently, but honestly, tells you that you are doing something incorrectly, don't take it personally. Be humble and do whatever it takes to correct your performance. If you want to take something personally, then do so when a child you are working with speaks his first word or is able to go to school for the first time because of the work you did. Or when an adult with autism is able to independently cook a meal for the first time or makes a new friend because of the social skills you taught him. But you are only going to produce these amazing outcomes if you do your job with a high degree of accuracy, and that is only going to happen if you are able to take feedback and learn from it.

Your supervisor will also help you set goals to improve your performance on an ongoing basis. For example, your supervising BCBA may work with you to develop short- and long-term performance goals such as delivering immediate and contingent reinforcement, implementing function-based extinction, collecting accurate data on behavior reduction targets, and running a learner's skill acquisition targets regularly. Your supervisor must then check back in with you after you have had time to improve your performance (e.g., 1 or 2 weeks) and evaluate whether you have met those goals. She will then give you specific feedback on how well you met those goals and then potentially set new goals for you. At first, it may seem like there must be something wrong with your performance if your supervisor needs to set goals for you. However, ongoing goal setting and feedback on behavior technician performance is just a regular part of top-quality ongoing supervision and it is essential to help you improve your skills on an ongoing basis.

7.3.3 Stakeholder Communication

You will often be put in positions to communicate with other stakeholders, including parents, caregivers, and staff from other agencies or schools. Keep in mind that, as a behavior technician, your job is to be the implementer, not the decision maker. So if a stakeholder asks you questions that are not within your role to answer, politely let the person know that you will ask the supervising BCBA to contact them with an answer. Questions that might not be appropriate for you to answer include questions about the rationale or justification behind a particular plan or procedure, how a particular procedure might be modified, the future plans or directions of a learner's intervention plan, in-depth questions about the research behind procedures, questions about the ethical justification for particular procedures, and many more. Fig. 7.2 lists some common questions stakeholders might ask you. Write out how you might respond to each question and ask your trainer for feedback on your answers. Stakeholder questions that are generally appropriate for you to answer are questions about general ABA concepts, such as the definition and purpose of using positive reinforcement, the importance of client dignity, the goal of fostering maximum independence, and so on. A good rule of thumb is that if you are not sure if it is appropriate for you to answer a question, you are probably better off telling the stakeholder that you will make sure your supervising BCBA gets back to them with the answer.

Stakeholder Question	Possible Response
A parent asks, "What do you think of the new behavior technician, is she any good?"	
A father says, "Jimmyhas to go to time out for that, put him in time out" (timeout is not part of the behavior reduction plan)	
You are modeling a program for school staff and they say, "When I worked at my old school/company we did it this other way. Why are you running it that way?"	
A parent approaches you at the end of your shift and says, "He has really seemed to regress, what do you think?"	
A parent asks, "What do you think of the speech pathologist that is doing his speech at school/outside speech, are they any good?"	
A family member asks, "What is your stance on (politics, abortion, religion)?"	
A teacher asks, "How do you like working at your school/agency?"	
A family member asks, "Do you think my child has a chance at recovering from autism?"	
A parent asks "What do you think of the special diet/vitamin supplements we are trying?"	

Figure 7.2 Difficult questions commonly asked by stakeholders. Write out potential responses and get feedback from your trainer on how you did. Reprinted with permission from Autism Bridges, Inc.

One very important general principle to consider is that, whenever you are communicating with stakeholders, you are the face of the agency or school for whom you work. Even though you are working in an entry-level position and do not have the authority to make major decisions, you are the one that others see on a regular basis and so you are the one who is going to make a lasting impression. For this reason, it is especially important for you to conduct yourself professionally and courteously around all other stakeholders. It is a cliché but the "golden rule" is a great guiding principle in these interactions. When you interact with a caregiver or another professional, how would you like them to treat you? Most everyone would like to be greeted with eye contact, a smile, and a courteous greeting. Taking a minute to make innocent small talk and ask how the person is doing can go a long way toward building positive working relationships with others. Of course, keep in mind, you are there to do a job with the learner, so be careful not to let small talk take longer than a minute or two because it will then rob the learner of precious session time.

One very common type of question that parents or caregivers often ask is about other learners with whom you work. Particularly in smaller towns and cities, families of your various clients may know each other and may try to talk to you about other families. It is absolutely imperative that you do not breach the confidentiality of one learner's family by talking about them to another learner's family. In such cases, you can neither confirm nor deny that you even know who they are talking about. You can politely say something like, "Federal privacy laws do not allow us to talk about our clients, so I cannot discuss whether I even know that person. Sorry to be so strict but I keep clients' confidentiality in the strictest of confidence and do the very same for your child," and then politely change the subject. It is worth remembering that federal HIPAA laws include serious fines and even jail-time for intentionally breaching client confidentiality.

7.3.4 Professional Boundaries

Working as a behavior technician with individuals with autism very often puts you in close contact with family members of the learner, often for prolonged periods of time. Especially if you work in a home-based program, you will often find that the learner's parents or other family members start to treat you as though you are a family member. Of course, it is nice for you and the family members to treat one another courteously, but it is important for you to keep the relationship professional. There is a very large potential for the family members of the learner to turn your relationship into something other than just a professional relationship. According to the *Professional and Ethical Compliance Code for Behavior Analysts*, a *multiple relationship* is "one in which a behavior analyst is in both a behavior-analytic role and a non- behavior-analytic role simultaneously with a client, supervisee, or someone closely associated with or related to the client" (Behavior Analyst Certification Board, 2014b). Multiple relationships can be harmful because a learner and her family are inherently in a vulnerable position in their relationship with you because they depend on you to care for their family member. If you entered into a multiple relationship with a family member and then the second relationship ended badly, it is very likely that the family member would feel uncomfortable with receiving behavioral services from you. In a very extreme example, if you entered into a sexual relationship with the parent of a child with autism who you were treating, and then the sexual relationship ended badly, that parent may never feel comfortable with seeing you again, let alone allowing you to work with his or her child.

Sexual or romantic relationships are obvious forms of multiple relationships and are very easy to avoid. You know when you are entering into one and you simply cannot do it. But other forms of multiple relationships are less obvious and can still be harmful. For example, if a parent of an individual with autism with whom you are working invites you to dinner with them after a session one day, it may seem innocent enough, and if that was all that was going to happen, then it might not be harmful. But if you go to dinner once and you both enjoy yourselves, then a more significant friendship may develop, even if it is not a romantic one. If you then become regular friends with the parent, it can become very difficult to do what you need to do as a behavior technician if you are also friends with the parent. For example, the parent may expect you to consume a celebratory drink with them before or after a session or they may invite you to go on vacations with them and you may feel obligated to go, even though it would not be appropriate.

Social media is a common source for potential multiple relationships. Many people are very liberal with who they "friend" on social media and who they allow to friend them. This may be harmless in your personal life, but it is a major potential source for multiple relationships and for unprofessional interactions. It is very common for people to post unprofessional pictures of themselves on social media sites and you do not want to invite the potential for misunderstanding or the development of multiple relationships. For these reasons, it is important to avoid friending clients on social media.

For all of the reasons described above, and many more, multiple relationships can be harmful and they should be avoided. The BACB

Professional and Ethical Compliance Code for Behavior Analysts clearly states the importance of avoiding multiple relationships:

1. Due to the potentially harmful effects of multiple relationships, behavior analysts avoid multiple relationships.
2. Behavior analysts must always be sensitive to the potentially harmful effects of multiple relationships. If behavior analysts find that, due to unforeseen factors, a multiple relationship has arisen, they seek to resolve it. (BACB, 2014)

If you are not sure if a particular behavior or activity might enter you into a multiple relationship, do not do the behavior, consult the *Professional and Ethical Compliance Code for Behavior Analysts*, and talk to your supervising BCBA immediately. In these cases, it is almost always "better to be safe than sorry." Once you have entered into a multiple relationship, it is often very difficult to remove yourself from it without hurting the feelings of the other person.

7.3.5 Client Dignity

When working as a behavior technician, it is critical to respect the dignity of those with whom you work, particularly the client and her family. A good general rule for respecting client dignity is that you should treat the client in the same manner that you would like to be treated if you had autism and you were receiving services from others. Another good rule of thumb is that you should treat the client in the manner in which you would want your brother, sister or your child treated if he or she was a client with autism.

In addition, there are many specific guidelines that are worth considering when maintaining client dignity. First, you should use respectful language when addressing the learner and went talking about her to others. It is good practice to place the person before the label. For example, talking about Ricky as a person with autism generally sounds more respectful and dignified than talking about Ricky as an autistic person (though certain communities within the autism population prefer the latter). Another good rule of thumb is to simply not label the diagnosis any more often than is needed. It is not shameful or bad in anyway to discuss a person's diagnosis of autism but it is also not necessary to discuss that person as a person with autism anymore than is actually needed for the purposes of effective communication. For example, when discussing Johnny's preferences, it is far more respectful to say, "Johnny loves lining up objects" than it is to say, "Johnny has autism so he loves lining up objects." In addition, do not label someone with one of their inappropriate behaviors. For example, do not call someone "a spitter," "a biter," or say that he is being "stimmy."

A crucial point to remember when maintaining client dignity is that many individuals with autism may not have the ability to advocate for themselves, so they may suffer mistreatment or humiliation in silence. Therefore, as a behavior technician, it is your job to look for ways in which your clients or students may be experiencing something nonpreferred or undignified merely because they do not have the ability to tell you so. For example, when assisting individuals with autism in their daily living routines, be sure to incorporate choice as often as possible so the individual herself can have the opportunity to have the greatest control over her own life as possible (review chapter: Behavior Reduction, for incorporating choice).

The learner's physical appearance is another important point to consider regarding client dignity. Again, using yourself or your own family member as a rule of thumb works well. Would you want your child or your sister walking around with food on her face or with her hair in a mess or her clothing dirty, stained, or disheveled? Even when the learner, herself, may not care about her appearance, her family and others very likely do, so it is important that you take that seriously. It is also very much worth considering that, if the individual with ASD does not have the language to tell you that they care about something, *it does not necessarily mean that they don't.* It simply means you do not know and it is far better to err on the side of taking precautions to respect others' dignity too much rather than too little.

It is also very worth considering the possibility that you do not have all of the information you need at any given point in time to make the learner comfortable. For example, if he is engaging in problematic behavior, your first thought should be to rule out any physical source of discomfort, hunger, sleep deprivation, and so on. Just like with everything else in ABA, we do not blame the learner, we blame the environment. Your first thought should always be to find what is happening in the environment that is responsible for the misbehavior the learner is displaying.

Learner independence is another critically important point to consider in relation to client dignity. Although the learners we work with often require support to function on a daily basis, our job is to increase independence to the greatest extent possible. It is very common to see individuals with autism who become unhappy when excessive prompting or direction is used. Generally speaking, you should always be looking for opportunities to step back, give the individual some space, and allow him or her to function independently, whenever it is safe and productive to do so. Remember, our job is to help the learner maximize independence and happiness by facilitating learning and by fading out prompting and support to the greatest degree possible.

7.4 STRESS AND BURNOUT

Now that you are nearly done with this manual and you have invested this much time into your training, we thought that we ought to be honest with you and let you know that you are in for some tough work ahead. The job that you have volunteered for is not an easy one. There will undoubtedly be days when you wonder why you chose such a challenging job. There may even be times when you feel like giving up. We are here to tell you that those are all normal human thoughts and emotions when you are in the thick of a tough challenge. And as you have already come this far, we are guessing that you chose this job for a reason—and that this job chose you for a reason. We are guessing that you are here because you are willing to work hard in order to make a difference for others who really need you. If that is the case, then you have come to the right place. If you are willing to give a lot of yourself, this job is going to give a lot back. Nothing we can write in this book will take the stress away. But we can give one small piece of wisdom: It is completely normal to feel tired, stressed out, and to feel like you never have it all figured out. And in case you are wondering how other behavior technicians seem to be doing just fine, they aren't. They are facing some of the toughest challenges of their careers, too. But they show up, every day. The difference between an excellent behavior technician who turns a passion into a job and a job into a career versus one who burns out is not whether they are tired, hesitant, or stressed. It is in what they choose to do while they have those difficult thoughts and feelings. If you are wondering when you are going to feel like this job is easy, you can stop wondering because it never really gets easy—there is always more to learn. But the good news is, the job does not need to feel like it is easy in order for you to give it your all. So, if you can, try to make room for your stress and your fatigue and still do the behaviors that you know matter, so you can make a real difference for the families you work with and so you can move one step closer to a career from which you can gain true satisfaction.

7.5 CONCLUSION

Congratulations! You have finished reading your behavior technician training manual and you have taken your first major step toward an incredibly rewarding career of making a real difference in the lives of other people. You have learned about some of the basic philosophical assumptions of ABA, including the belief that all people are capable of learning and that all individuals with disabilities have a right to the most effective and least intrusive treatment. You have learned some basic information about autism and some of the research that supports ABA treatment, both focused and comprehensive.

You have learned how to measure behavior, including the importance of data collection, and how to record data using frequency/rate, duration, partial interval, and momentary time sampling, to name a few. You have learned about the basic principles of learning and motivation that form the foundation of ABA, including reinforcement, extinction, stimulus control, generalization, and many more. Most importantly, you have learned how the basic principles of ABA can be used to help individuals with autism decrease their challenging behaviors and replace them with more appropriate skills. Finally, you have learned about the importance of documentation and professionalism, including maintaining client dignity.

You now have the foundational knowledge you need to make a difference, while working under the supervision of a BCBA. But don't forget, all the knowledge in the world is useless if you don't know how to put it to use! So get out there and practice, practice, practice! Get the best quality supervision you can from top-quality BCBAs who are experts in autism treatment, and demand ongoing supervision and professional growth. Remember, you cannot get top-quality results if you put in average quality effort. Give it your all and insist on the best from your colleagues and peers. Go forth and do amazing things with what you have learned. You truly can make a difference!

Sample Skill Acquisition Ideas Sheet*

F I R S T S T E P S

early intervention program

IMAGINARY PLAY IDEAS

CREATING IMAGINARY WORLDS WITHOUT PROPS

Now that the Child has practiced pretend play with "Functional" and "Symbolic" objects, we're going to explore the joys of play without props. "Imaginary Play," or using language and gestures to represent "not present" objects | people | locations | properties and the like, takes pretend play to the next level!

IMAGINARY ACTIONS + OBJECTS

One of the simplest ways to start exploring Imaginary Play is in pretending to do simple "actions" with imaginary (or invisible) "objects"—basically, "charades" or "miming," but sound effects and talking are all good (and encouraged)! The Imaginary Play Program Plan lists a variety of common ones, but to get your "acting chops" moving, think:

- Eating "Food" • Playing "Guitar" • "Flying" • Carrying a "Ball"

Imaginary Properties

Once the Child is doing actions with "Imaginary Objects," we'll practice ways to make the play even more rich. One of these is discussing

---

*Reprinted with permission from FirstSteps for Kids, Inc.

"Imaginary Properties." For example, we model and encourage tacting of "creative" elements such as:

- *Size*: Imaginary cookies can be "teeny tiny," a giraffe is "taller than the whole house!"
- *Weight*: Carry imaginary boxes that are "really heavy" or "so light"
- *Temperature*: Imaginary snowballs are "freezing cold," pretend food is "too hot"
- *Texture*: After getting splashed with imaginary water, we'll be "soaking wet"
- *Emotions*: Imaginary friends might be "happy" or "sad"

Responding to Others' Imagination

Part of imaginary play is not just coming up with your own ideas, but responding to what others are doing as well. Some example ideas include:

- *Catching* an imaginary "ball" when someone throws it (then throwing it back!)
- *Looking* at imaginary creatures when someone points to them across the room
- *Slipping and Sliding* on the imaginary ice that someone froze on the ground
- *Sipping* the imaginary tea someone just brewed for you ... etc.

IMAGINARY LOCATIONS | THEMES

Imaginary Locations

One of the most fun experiences Imaginary Play offers is the ability to "visit" favorite places and "travel" to far off lands and exotic locales, all without leaving the house! Work with the Child on "touring" locations, talking about what he "sees"—"who's" there, what's "happening," and so on.

Imaginary Themes

Once the Child is "seeing" the sights at Imaginary Locations, the stage is set to combine Imaginary Actions, Objects, and Properties (as well as previous Functional Pretend and Symbolic targets) in multiple-step thematic play scenarios using language and gestures. Some example themes include:

- *The Beach*: Lay out a "towel," feel the "hot sun," dive in the "ocean," "surf," get knocked over by a "wave," look at the "birds" flying overhead, and so on.
- *Zoo*: Buy "tickets," walk around looking at different "animals," feed "peanuts" to the "elephants," run away from the "scary tigers" etc.
- *Mountains*: Drive a "car" up a "winding road," smell the "fresh air," build a "campfire," "warm" cold hands at the "fire," watch the "squirrels" climb the trees, build a "tent," etc.

Ethical Guidelines

The following ethical guidelines are quoted verbatim from the outline of the *Professional and Ethical Compliance Code for Behavior Analysts* (Behavior Analyst Certification Board, 2014).

1.0 RESPONSIBLE CONDUCT OF BEHAVIOR ANALYSTS

1.01 Reliance on Scientific Knowledge RBT
1.02 Boundaries of Competence RBT
1.03 Maintaining Competence through Professional Development RBT
1.04 Integrity RBT
1.05 Professional and Scientific Relationships RBT
1.06 Multiple Relationships and Conflicts of Interest RBT
1.07 Exploitative Relationships RBT

2.0 BEHAVIOR ANALYSTS' RESPONSIBILITY TO CLIENTS

2.01 Accepting Clients
2.02 Responsibility RBT
2.03 Consultation
2.04 Third-Party Involvement in Services
2.05 Rights and Prerogatives of Clients RBT
2.06 Maintaining Confidentiality RBT
2.07 Maintaining Records RBT
2.08 Disclosures RBT
2.09 Treatment/Intervention Efficacy
2.10 Documenting Professional Work and Research RBT
2.11 Records and Data RBT
2.12 Contracts, Fees, and Financial Arrangements
2.13 Accuracy in Billing Reports
2.14 Referrals and Fees
2.15 Interrupting or Discontinuing Services

3.0 ASSESSING BEHAVIOR

3.01 Behavior-Analytic Assessment RBT
3.02 Medical Consultation
3.03 Behavior-Analytic Assessment Consent
3.04 Explaining Assessment Results
3.05 Consent-Client Records

4.0 BEHAVIOR ANALYSTS AND THE BEHAVIOR-CHANGE PROGRAM

4.01 Conceptual Consistency
4.02 Involving Clients in Planning and Consent
4.03 Individualized Behavior-Change Programs
4.04 Approving Behavior-Change Programs
4.05 Describing Behavior-Change Program Objectives
4.06 Describing Conditions for Behavior-Change Program Success
4.07 Environmental Conditions that Interfere with Implementation
4.08 Considerations Regarding Punishment Procedures
4.09 Least Restrictive Procedures
4.10 Avoiding Harmful Reinforcers RBT
4.11 Discontinuing Behavior-Change Programs and Behavior-Analytic Services

5.0 BEHAVIOR ANALYSTS AS SUPERVISORS

5.01 Supervisory Competence
5.02 Supervisory Volume
5.03 Supervisory Delegation
5.04 Designing Effective Supervision and Training
5.05 Communication of Supervision Conditions
5.06 Providing Feedback to Supervisees
5.07 Evaluating the Effects of Supervision

6.0 BEHAVIOR ANALYSTS' ETHICAL RESPONSIBILITY TO THE PROFESSION OF BEHAVIOR ANALYSTS

6.01 Affirming Principles RBT
6.02 Disseminating Behavior Analysis RBT

7.0 BEHAVIOR ANALYSTS' ETHICAL RESPONSIBILITY TO COLLEAGUES

7.01 Promoting an Ethical Culture RBT

7.02 Ethical Violations by Others and Risk of Harm RBT

8.0 PUBLIC STATEMENTS

8.01 Avoiding False or Deceptive Statements RBT

8.02 Intellectual Property RBT

8.03 Statements by Others RBT

8.04 Media Presentations and Media-Based Services

8.05 Testimonials and Advertising RBT

8.06 In-Person Solicitation RBT

9.0 BEHAVIOR ANALYSTS AND RESEARCH

9.01 Conforming with Laws and Regulations RBT

9.02 Characteristics of Responsible Research

9.03 Informed Consent

9.04 Using Confidential Information for Didactic or Instructive Purposes

9.05 Debriefing

9.06 Grant and Journal Reviews

9.07 Plagiarism

9.08 Acknowledging Contributions

9.09 Accuracy and Use of Data RBT

10.0 BEHAVIOR ANALYSTS' ETHICAL RESPONSIBILITY TO THE BACB

10.01 Truthful and Accurate Information Provided to the BACB RBT

10.02 Timely Responding, Reporting, and Updating of Information Provided to the BACB RBT

10.03 Confidentiality and BACB Intellectual Property RBT

10.04 Examination Honesty and Irregularities RBT

10.05 Compliance with BACB Supervision and Coursework Standards RBT

10.06 Being Familiar with This Code

10.07 Discouraging Misrepresentation by Non-Certified Individuals RBT

APPENDIX *C*

Sample Field Evaluation*

BEHAVIOR TECHNICIAN COMPETENCY EXAM—SCHOOL BASED VERSION

F-02 Respond appropriately to feedback and maintain or improve performance accordingly *The candidate is informed of this requirement at the onset of the competency exam.*

Scenarios:

1. During feedback sessions with the supervisor, the candidate will respond by accepting feedback (e.g., saying thank you, asking questions for clarification), state a plan to maintain or improve performance on another occasion, and manage any emotional response (e.g., no crying).

Administration process:

1. Provide the candidate with feedback regarding performance throughout the assessment.

Passing Criteria:

1. The candidate will display acceptable behaviors specified above (e.g., questions for clarification, a plan for maintaining and improving performance).

A-02 IMPLEMENT CONTINUOUS MEASUREMENT PROCEDURES

Scenarios (complete at least one):

1. *While observing in a classroom, the candidate will record <u>teacher reprimand statements</u> (i.e., any vocal or gestural statement that reflects*

---

*Reprinted With Permission From Shawn Quigley.

disapproval of student behavior [e.g., "Do not do that," "Those are naughty hands," frown, stink eye]) or praise statements (i.e., using any vocal or gestural statements that reflects approval of student behavior [e.g., "Nice job," "I like your work," thumbs up, high-five]) using a frequency count. The observation period is 2-m in length.

   a. Using the information from the above scenario, the candidate can also calculate rate of reprimand or praise statements.

2. While observing in a classroom, the candidate will record student talking (i.e., any vocal statement or noise emitted by one student) using a duration measure. The observation period is 3-m in length.

   a. Using the information from the above scenario, the candidate can calculate a total duration, frequency count with total duration, or percent of total interval where the target behavior occurred.

Administration process:

1. Instruct the candidate to record teacher reprimand statements for 2-minutes using frequency count recording. Provide the definition for teacher reprimand statements. No further information should be provided but the instructions can be repeated. The supervisor will follow the same procedures and generate his/her own data.

2. Instruct the candidate to record student talking for 3-minutes using duration recording. Provide the definition for student talking. No further information should be provided but the instructions can be repeated. The supervisor will follow the same procedures and generate his/her own data.

Passing Criteria:

The candidate and supervisor will compare data from the scenario using a point-by-point agreement method (i.e., scenario #1) or a percent agreement procedure (i.e., scenario #2). The candidate must have at least 80% agreement with the supervisor to pass.

COMPLETE ONLY ONE – A-03 or A-04

A-03* IMPLEMENT DISCONTINUOUS MEASUREMENT PROCEDURES

Scenarios (complete at least one):

1. While observing in a classroom, the candidate will record teacher reprimand statements (i.e., any vocal or gestural statement that reflects disapproval of student behavior [e.g., "Do not do that,"

"Those are naughty hands," frown, stink eye]) or <u>*teacher praise*</u> <u>*statements*</u> *(i.e., any vocal or gestural statement that reflects approval of student behavior [e.g., "Good job", "Nice working", thumbs up, high five]) using* <u>*10-s partial interval*</u> *recording.*

2. *While observing in a classroom, the candidate will measure* <u>*teacher*</u> <u>*talking*</u> *(i.e., any vocal statements or noises [e.g., screaming, humming] emitted by the teacher]) using* <u>*10-s whole interval*</u> *recording.*

3. *While observing in a classroom, the candidate will record* <u>*student on-*</u> <u>*task behavior*</u> *(i.e., eyes toward work, vocal/gestural responses that are related to the task, eyes on the teacher) using* <u>*30-s momentary*</u> <u>*time-sampling*</u> *recording.*

Administration process:

1. *Instruct the candidate to record* <u>*teacher praise statements*</u> *for 1-minute using 10-s partial interval recording. Provide the definition for teacher praise statements. No further information should be provided but the instructions can be repeated. The supervisor will follow the same procedures and generate his/her own data.*

2. *Instruct the candidate to record* <u>*teacher talking*</u> *for 1-minute using 10-s whole interval recording. Provide the definition for teacher talking. No further information should be provided but the instructions can be repeated. The supervisor will follow the same procedures and generate his/her own data.*

3. *Instruct the candidate to record* <u>*student on-task behavior*</u> *for 3-minutes using 30-s momentary time-sampling recording. Provide the definition for student on-task behavior. No further information should be provided but the instructions can be repeated. The supervisor will follow the same procedures and generate his/her own data.*

Passing Criteria:

The candidate and supervisor will compare data from the scenario using a point-by-point agreement method. The candidate must have at least 80% agreement with the supervisor to pass.

A-04* IMPLEMENT PERMANENT PRODUCT RECORDING PROCEDURES

Scenario:

After students have completed a classroom assignment that results in a permanent product (e.g., spelling test, report, wood project, sorted objects), the candidate will assess whether the product met the pre-established passing criteria (e.g., >30 correct responses per minute, >80% match-to-sample accuracy).

Administration process:

Instruct the candidate to evaluate whether or not the permanent product met the pre-established passing criteria.

Passing criteria:

The candidate correctly stated if the permanent product met the pre-established passing criteria. Also, the candidate correctly stated what features of the permanent product were correct and which features were incorrect.

A-05 ENTER DATA AND UPDATE GRAPHS

Scenario:

The candidate will plot the data from Tasks A-02 and A-03 on an equal interval graph.

Administration process:

Instruct the candidate to plot data obtained from Task A-02 and A-03. The graph must include a graph title, axis labels, axis scales and connected data points.

Passing criteria:

The candidate must plot the data and label all parts of a graph with 100% accuracy.

B-02 CONDUCT PREFERENCE ASSESSMENTS

Scenarios (complete at least two):

1. *The candidate will conduct a free operant preference assessment with a student in the classroom. The candidate will conduct the assessment in the typical classroom setting. The candidate will record responses and report a preference hierarchy.*
2. *The candidate will conduct a forced-choice preference assessment with a student in the classroom. The candidate will use six stimuli*

typically available in the classroom setting. The candidate will record responses and report a preference hierarchy.

3. *The candidate will conduct a <u>multiple choice with replacement</u> prefer- ence assessment with a student in the classroom. The candidate will use six stimuli typically available in the classroom setting. The candi- date will record responses and report a preference hierarchy.*

4. *The candidate will conduct a <u>multiple choice without replacement</u> preference assessment with a student in the classroom. The candidate will use six stimuli typically available in the classroom setting. The candidate will record responses and report a preference hierarchy.*

Administration process:

Have the candidate obtain the data sheet, writing utensil and stimuli. Instruct the candidate to conduct one of the preference assessments. No further information should be provided but the instructions can be repeated. The supervisor will use the appropriate preference assessment fidelity sheet for each assessment (i.e., setup, administration of choices, inter-trial interval, recording of choices, setup for subsequent choices, determining preference hierarchy). The supervisor will also indepen- dently generate his/her own data for later comparison.

Passing criteria:

The candidate must administer two different preference assessments with 80% fidelity on each assessment.

B-04 ASSIST WITH FUNCTIONAL ASSESSMENT PROCEDURES

Scenarios (complete at least one):

1. *While observing in a classroom, the candidate will provide a <u>narrative record</u> of one student's behavior (i.e., continuous description of ABCs at the onset of the observation). The observation period is 5-m in length.*

2. *While observing in a classroom, the candidate will record a predeter- mined <u>target behavior for a student</u> (i.e., an operational definition must be provided and discussed prior to beginning) using <u>ABC recording</u> procedures. The observation period is 5-m in length.*

Administration process:

1. *Instruct the candidate to record ABCs of the classroom for 5-minutes in a <u>narrative format</u>. No further information should be provided but*

the instructions can be repeated. The supervisor will follow the same procedures and generate his/her own record.

2. *Instruct the candidate to record the predetermined <u>target behavior</u> for 5-minutes using an ABC format. No further information should be provided but the instructions can be repeated. The supervisor will follow the same procedures and generate his/her own record.*

Passing Criteria:

1. *The candidate and supervisor will compare data from the <u>narrative recording</u> scenario. The candidate will summarize key antecedent events occurring before student and teacher behavior, socially inappropriate teacher and student behaviors and key consequences that may be maintaining the socially inappropriate behaviors. The candidate must have at least 80% agreement with the supervisor's key ABC points to pass. When determining agreement, consider factors such as ability to see certain response (e.g., supervisor view blocked by another student) and language (e.g., using different words to convey similar meaning).*

2. *The candidate and supervisor will compare data from the <u>ABC recording</u> on a point-by-point basis. The candidate must have at least 80% agreement with the supervisor's data. When determining agreement, consider factors such as ability to see certain response (e.g., supervisor view blocked by another student) and language (e.g., using different words to convey similar meaning).*

C-03 USE CONTINGENCIES OF REINFORCEMENT

Scenarios (complete at least one):

1. *While providing individual, small group, or large group instruction, <u>praise</u> students on a <u>continuous schedule</u> for accurate work and socially acceptable classroom behavior (e.g., raising hand).*

2. *While providing individual, small group, or large group instruction, <u>praise</u> students on an <u>intermittent schedule</u> for accurate work and socially acceptable classroom behavior (e.g., raising hand).*

3. *While providing individual, small group, or large group instruction, use the classroom <u>token economy</u> (e.g., points, marbles in a jar)on a <u>continuous schedule</u> for accurate work and socially acceptable classroom behavior (e.g., raising hand).*

4. *While providing individual, small group, or large group instruction, use the classroom <u>token economy</u> (e.g., points, marbles in a jar) on*

an   intermittent   schedule   for   accurate   work   and   socially acceptable classroom behavior (e.g., raising hand).

Administration Process:

Give the above instruction (choose one) and follow for no longer than ten minutes.

Passing Criteria:

The candidate implements the contingency with at least 80% accuracy as measured by administrator rating.

†COMPLETE ONLY ONE – C-04, C-05 or C-06†

C-04† IMPLEMENT DISCRETE TRIAL TRAINING PROCEDURES

Scenario:

1. *The candidate presents ten match-to-sample trials (or other learning activity more appropriate for the student) using a discrete trial format.*

Administration Process:

1. *Instruct the candidate to present ten match-to-sample trials (or other learning activity more appropriate for the student) using a discrete trial format.*

Passing Criteria:

1. *The candidate must perform the trials with at least 80% accuracy based upon the discrete trial fidelity form (i.e., trial setup, gaining student attention, salient Sd, prompting procedures, correct procedures for correct and incorrect response, inter-trial interval, setup for subsequent trials).*

C-05† IMPLEMENT NATURALISTIC TEACHING PROCEDURES

Scenario:

1. *While interacting with peers, the candidate instructs a student on a social skill (or other learning activity more appropriate for the student) using a naturalistic teaching format.*

Administration Process:

1. *Instruct the candidate to teach a social skill (or other learning activity more appropriate for the student) using a naturalistic teaching format.*

Passing Criteria:

1. *The candidate provides instruction with at least 80% accuracy based upon the naturalistic teaching fidelity form (i.e., captures natural motivation, gains student attention, indicates natural Sd, prompting/ modeling procedures, links correct and incorrect responses to natural contingencies, uses contrived contingencies as necessary).*

C-06† IMPLEMENT TASK ANALYZED CHAINING PROCEDURES

Scenario:

1. *A student is learning a new play skill. The candidate will use a backward chaining procedure to complete a simple Lego® toy.*

Administration Process:

1. *Instruct the candidate to teach a Lego® play skill by using a backward chaining procedure.*

Passing Criteria:

1. *The candidate implements the intervention with at least 80% accuracy based upon observation (i.e., has materials ready, gains student attention, provides Sd for final task, prompting/modeling procedures, play with toy based upon correct response, contrived contingency to support play, repeat of steps with additional steps of task analysis required).*

   COMPLETE ONLY ONE – C-07, C-08, C-09 or C-10

C-07* IMPLEMENT DISCRIMINATION TRAINING

Scenarios (complete at least one):

1. *The candidate will use two different stimuli (e.g., color disks) to teach discriminated responses with a student. The candidate will train*

the student to talk in the presence of one stimulus and work independently in the presence of the other stimulus.

Administration Process:

1. *Give two stimuli to the candidate and instruct him/her to train a student to talk in the presence of one stimulus and work independently in the presence of the other stimulus.*

Passing Criteria:

1. *The candidate creates a context in which the desired behavior (i.e., talking and working independently) is reinforced in the presence of one stimulus and extinguished in the presence of the second stimulus. The candidate must implement the procedure with at least 80% fidelity according to the discrimination training fidelity form (i.e., discriminative stimuli, use of rules as appropriate, correct reinforcement and extinction procedures in the presence of the correct Sd).*

C-08* IMPLEMENT STIMULUS CONTROL TRANSFER PROCEDURES

Scenario:

1. *When teaching students to read sight words, the candidate will use an echoic to tact transfer procedure.*

Administration Process:

1. *Instruct the candidate to use a deck of cards with sight words written on them to teach a student the words. The candidate is to use an echoic to tact transfer procedure.*

Passing Criteria:

1. *The candidate implements the procedure with 80% or better fidelity as measured by the echoic to tact fidelity form (i.e., present card with echoic cue, "Say _____" [echoic component], vocal prompting if necessary, contingency for correct response, "What does it say" [tact component], prompting if necessary, contingency for correct response).*

C-09* IMPLEMENT STIMULUS FADING PROCEDURES

Scenario:

1. *While teaching money recognition (or other learning activity more appropriate for the student) the candidate uses stimulus-based prompts to increase accurate responding.*

Administration Process:

1. *Instruct the candidate to teach money recognition using differentially sized coins in a match-to-sample format. The candidate should fade the size prompt of the sample stimuli and matching stimuli based upon student performance.*

Passing Criteria:

1. *The candidate reduces size prompts after each correct response or at a slower pace if the prompt reduction leads to increased errors. The focus of the procedure is an ability to reduce stimulus prompts, recognize the effect upon student responding, and adjusting as necessary.*

C-10* IMPLEMENT PROMPT AND PROMPT FADING PROCEDURES

Scenario:

1. *The candidate presents several match-to-sample trials (or other learning activity more appropriate for the student) using a most-to-least prompt procedure within a discrete trial format.*

Administration Process:

1. *Instruct the candidate to present several match-to-sample trials using a most-to-least prompt procedure within a discrete trial format. The candidate fades the prompt with each new trial (or as quickly as possible given student performance).*

Passing Criteria:

1. *The candidate utilizes less obtrusive prompts after each correct response or at a slower pace if the prompt reduction leads to increased errors. The focus of the procedure is an ability to reduce prompts, recognize the effect upon student responding, and adjusting*

as necessary. Observing an actual stimulus control transfer might not be possible within the limited trials of the assessment.

†COMPLETE ONLY ONE – D-03, D-04, or D-05†

D-03† IMPLEMENT INTERVENTIONS BASED ON MODIFICATION OF ANTECEDENTS

Scenario:

1. *A teacher is working on the frequency of appropriate mands with a student. The student often tantrums when a toy is not available.*

Administration process:

1. *The candidate should identify various preferred toys for a student. The candidate should demonstrate how to create a motivating context for the student to request one of the toys.*

Passing Criteria:

1. *The candidate must arrange a motivating context for the student to mand (e.g., places the toys just out of reach, establishes "play time" via a discriminative stimulus). The candidate uses appropriate prompts to encourage the desired mand response (e.g., vocal, picture exchange, sign) and to decrease the use of undesirable mand responses (i.e., tantrum).*

D-04† IMPLEMENT DIFFERENTIAL REINFORCEMENT AND EXTINCTION PROCEDURES (LIVE)

Scenario:

1. *Varied based upon student needs*

Administration process:

1. *The examiner will determine an undesirable behavior that is appropriate for extinction and differential reinforcement procedures. The examiner will provide instructions for intervention using extinction and differential reinforcement.*

Passing Criteria:

1. *The candidate will implement the procedure with at least 80% fidelity as measured by observation (i.e., identification of function, definition*

of target behavior, definition of replacement behavior, no environmental changes in relation to target behavior, and functional environmental changes in relation to replacement behavior).

D-05† – IMPLEMENT DIFFERENTIAL REINFORCEMENT AND EXTINCTION PROCEDURES (ROLE PLAY)

Scenarios:

1. *A student frequently yells to get the teacher's attention. The teacher would like the student to learn a more appropriate way to get the teacher's attention.*

Administration process:

1. *The candidate will need to identify a replacement behavior, extinguish the target behavior, and reinforce the replacement behavior.*

Passing Criteria:

1. *The candidate will implement the procedure with at least 80% fidelity as measured by observation (i.e., definition of target behavior, definition of replacement behavior, no environmental changes in relation to target behavior, and functional environmental changes in relation to replacement behavior).*

Some school personnel are trained in program specific crisis/emergency procedures. Proof of training in the procedure is required from an approved source (e.g., trainer, district human resource office). Non-trained staff are expected to follow district policy for requesting crisis/emergency support.

D-06 IMPLEMENT CRISIS/EMERGENCY PROCEDURES ACCORDING TO PROTOCOL (ROLE PLAY)

Scenarios:

1. A teacher has recently been trained in the school crisis/emergency procedures. The procedure is a multi-step process starting with verbal de-escalation (e.g., statements of empathy), reduction of demands, redirection to a preferred activity, rearrangement of

environment to keep everyone safe (e.g., furniture between the student and teacher), and physical management procedures.

Administration process:

1. The candidate is given the above scenario. The candidate must describe how the procedure can be implemented. The candidate must describe how a functional assessment and function-based intervention can prevent/reduce the need for crisis/emergency protocols. Additionally, the candidate must describe how an understanding of behavioral function might alter crisis/emergency protocols.

Passing criteria:

1. The candidate adequately describes the crisis/emergency procedures including functional assessment, intervention, and individualization of procedures based upon function. The candidate must clearly state what level of training they have and what role they play in crisis/emergency situations.

E-02 GENERATE OBJECTIVE SESSION NOTES BY DESCRIBING WHAT OCCURRED DURING SESSIONS

Scenarios:

1. *Using information from this assessment, the candidate will write an objective session note.*

Administration process:

1. *Instruct the candidate to complete a session note based on the SOAP format for one of the assessment sections (i.e., a note for all of Section A, Section B, Section C, or Section D). No further information should be provided but the instructions can be repeated.*
2. *The supervisor will also take notes based on the SOAP format.*

Passing Criteria:

1. *The SOAP notes will contain subjective information about the teaching session (student mood, motivation, timing, etc.) objective information related to performance, other behaviors, etc.; assessment of the teaching session (including candidate performance); how the session related to the teaching plan. The candidate notes will match the*

supervisor's notes on no less than three of four possible areas. When determining agreement, consider factors such as ability to see certain response (e.g., supervisor view blocked by another student) and language (e.g., using different words to convey similar meaning).

REFERENCES

American Psychiatric Association. (2013). *Diagnostic and statistical manual of mental disorders* (5th ed.). Washington, DC: Author.

Baer, D. M., Wolf, M. M., & Risley, T. R. (1968). Some current dimensions of applied behavior analysis. *Journal of Applied Behavior Analysis*, *1*, 91–97.

Behavior Analyst Certification Board. (2013). *Registered Behavior Technician™ (RBT™) Task List*. <http://bacb.com/wp-content/uploads/2016/03/160321-RBT-task-list.pdf>.

Behavior Analyst Certification Board. (2014a). *Applied behavior analysis treatment of autism spectrum disorder: Practice guidelines for healthcare funders and managers*. <http://bacb.com/wp-content/uploads/2015/07/ABA_Guidelines_for_ASD.pdf>.

Behavior Analyst Certification Board. (2014b). *Professional and ethical compliance code for behavior analysts*. <http://bacb.com/wp-content/uploads/2016/03/160321-compliance-code-english.pdf>.

Behavior Analyst Certification Board. (2016). *Registered Behavior Technician™ (RBT)™ Competency Assessment*. <http://bacb.com/wp-content/uploads/2016/01/160129-RBT-competency-assessment.pdf>.

Cooper, J. O. H., Heward, T. E., William, L., Cooper, J. O., Heron, T. E., & Heward, W. L. (2007). *Applied behavior analysis*. Upper Saddle River, NJ: Prentice Hall.

Dixon, M. (2015). *PEAK relational training system: Evidence-based autism assessment and treatment: Equivalence module*. Carbondale, IL: Shawnee Scientific Press.

Hanley, G. P., Iwata, B. A., & McCord, B. E. (2003). Functional analysis of problem behavior: A review. *Journal of Applied Behavior Analysis*, *36*(2), 147–185.

National Autism Center. (2015). *The National Standards Report*. Randolph, MA: National Autism Center.

Partington, J. W. (2008). *The Assessment of Basic Language and Learning Skills-Revised (The ABLLS-R)*. Pleasant Hill, CA: Behavior Analysts, Inc.

Quigley, S.P., Blevins, P., & Trott, M. (2016). *Behavior technician competency exam—School based version*. Unpublished Manuscript. Center for Development and Disability, University of New Mexico & New Mexico Department of Health.

Sundberg, M. L. (2008). *Verbal behavior milestones assessment and placement program: The VB-MAPP*. Concord, CA: AVBPress.

Tarbox, J., Dixon, D. R., Sturmey, P., & Matson, J. L. (Eds.), (2014). *Handbook of early intervention for autism spectrum disorders: Research, policy, and practice* New York, NY: Springer.

Wilke, A. E., Tarbox, J., Dixon, D. R., Kenzer, A. L., Bishop, M. R., & Kakavand, H. (2012). Indirect functional assessment of stereotypy in children with autism spectrum disorders. *Research in Autism Spectrum Disorders*, *6*(2), 824–828.

INDEX

Note: Page numbers followed by "*f*" and "*t*" refer to figures and tables, respectively.

A

Abolishing operations, 62
Analytic applied behavior analysis, 4
Antecedent-behavior-consequence (ABC) data,
  42–45
  narrative data, 43, 44*f*
  structured data, 44–45, 44*f*
Antecedent modifications, 89, 95–98
  choice, 98
  demand fading, 96–97
  high-probability, low-probability sequence,
    97–98
  interventions based on, implementing,
    143
  noncontingent reinforcement (NCR), 95–96
  task modification, 97
Applied behavior analysis (ABA), 1
  dimensions of, 3–5
  foundational principles, 5–9
Asperger's disorder, 12
Assessment, 35
  behavior and environment, observable and
    measurable descriptions
    of, 35–41
    frequent brief multiple stimulus
      preference assessment, 40–41
    identifying items to include preference
      assessment, 37
    multiple stimulus in preference
      assessment, 39–40, 40*f*
    paired choice preference assessment,
      37–39, 38*f*
    preference assessment, 36–37
    single item preference assessment, 37, 38*f*
  functional assessment procedures, 42–45
    antecedent-behavior-consequence data,
      42–45, 44*f*
  skill acquisition assessment procedures,
    41–42
    baseline/probing, 42
*Assessment of Basic Language and Learning
  Skills—Revised (ABLLS-R)*, 41
Attention extinction, 102–103
Attention function, 92–93

Autism spectrum disorder (ASD), 3, 11
  ABA treatment for, 15–18
    comprehensive treatment, 16
    focused treatment, 16–17
    general philosophy of programs, 17–18
  background of, 11–12
  diagnostic criteria for, 12–15
    DSM-5 criteria, 13–14
    severity, 14
  history of, 11–12
  myths and rumors, 14
Automatically reinforced behavior, extinction
  of, 105–106
Automatic reinforcement, 94–95
Average duration, 22

B

Backup reinforcers, 57
Backward chaining, 70
Baseline/probing, in skill acquisition
  assessment, 42
Behavioral applied behavior analysis, 3–4
Behavioral emergency, 91–92, 106
Behavioral momentum procedures.
  See High-probability, low-probability
    (high-p, low-p) sequence
Behavioral skills training (BST), 115
Behavior and environment, observable and
  measurable descriptions of, 35–41
Behavior intervention plan (BIP).
  See Behavior reduction plan
Behavior reduction, 89
  antecedent modifications, 95–98
    choice, 98
    demand fading, 96–97
    high-probability, low-probability
      sequence, 97–98
    noncontingent reinforcement (NCR),
      95–96
    task modification, 97
  crisis/emergency procedures, 106–107
    emergency behavior management
      training, 107

CPSIA information can be obtained
at www.ICGtesting.com
Printed in the USA
LVOW12s1616031117
554901LV00002B/339/P